COLLINS GEM

COOK'S RECKONER

The Diagram Group

HarperCollins*Publishers*

HarperCollins Publishers
P.O. Box, Glasgow G4 0NB

A Diagram book first created by Diagram Visual Information Limited of 195 Kentish Town Road, London NW5 8SY

First published 1997

Reprint 10 9 8 7 6 5 4 3 2 1 0

ISBN 0 00 472058-X

Printed in Great Britain by
Caledonian International Book Manufacturing Limited,
Glasgow G64

Introduction

What sort of ingredient is a 'doong gwooh'? What is the metric equivalent of 2 lb? How long can meat be stored in a freezer? What is meant by 'knocking up' pastry? These and many other questions are answered in *Collins Gem Cook's Reckoner*.

The book is divided into five sections. The first section includes conversion tables for metric and imperial units; they give both approximate or handy equivalents and exact ones. Section 2 defines cooking methods and unusual cooking ingredients from a wide range of international cuisines. Kitchen equipment and utensils are described in section 3, along with tips on usage. Section 4 provides information on buying, storing and cooking various types of food; there are also international wine quality classifications and tips for cooking with alcoholic drink. The final section, health and nutrition, gives advice on what to eat for a healthy balanced diet, along with information on food labels, food additives and calorie content.

With its clearly set out tables, easy-to-follow instructions and many useful tips, *Collins Gem Cook's Reckoner* is an invaluable, handy-sized companion in the kitchen.

Contents

8 Table finder

12 1. Weights and measures

12 Weight and volume measures

14 Weights
14 UK imperial and metric conversions

16 Liquid measures
16 UK imperial, US customary and metric conversions

20 Other volume measures
20 Water weights
21 Liquid and dry measures
22 Cups and spoonfuls

25 Temperature measures

26 2. Glossaries

26 Cooking methods and processes

38 Cooking ingredients

48 3. Equipment and utensils

48 Cookers

54 Refrigerators

58 Freezers

60 Food processing machines
62 Measuring and weighing equipment
65 Pots and pans
69 Knives and other cutting tools
73 Bakeware and moulds
76 Other hand tools

81 **4. Food and Drink**

82 Meat
82 Cuts of meat and cooking methods
87 Buying meat
87 Storing meat
90 Cooking meat

93 Poultry and game
93 Types of poultry and game
95 Buying poultry and game
98 Storing poultry and game
100 Cooking poultry and game

105 Seafood
105 Types of seafood
107 Buying seafood
111 Storing seafood
113 Cooking seafood

115 Vegetables and fruit
115 Types of vegetables
124 Types of fruit
129 Buying vegetables and fruit

132 Storing vegetables and fruit
136 Preserving fruit
138 Cooking vegetables

140 Nuts and pulses
140 Types of nuts
141 Types of pulses
142 Buying nuts and pulses
142 Storing nuts and pulses
143 Cooking pulses

144 Herbs and spices
144 Types of herbs and spices
150 Buying herbs and spices
150 Storing herbs and spices
151 Cooking with herbs and spices

151 Dairy products
151 Types of dairy milk
153 Types of egg
154 Types of cheese
156 Storing dairy products

159 Miscellaneous foods
159 Types of bread
160 Types of flour
161 Types of oil
164 Types of pasta
167 Types of rice
169 Types of sweeteners
171 Types of vegetarian alternatives
172 Buying and storing miscellaneous foods

175 Alcoholic drink

175 Types of alcoholic drink
177 Measuring alcoholic drink
178 Buying wine
183 Storing and serving wine
187 Cooking with alcoholic drink

188 Tea and coffee
188 Types of tea
190 Types of coffee
192 Storing tea and coffee

193 **5. Health and nutrition**

193 Proteins

195 Carbohydrates

196 Fats

200 Vitamins
202 Vitamin tables

208 Minerals
210 Mineral tables

218 Food and energy
219 Food and drink calorie table

228 Food additives
230 Food additives table

244 Food labels

248 Balancing your diet

251 **Index**

Table finder

Additives, food 230–45
Alcoholic units per standard measure 177

Bacon, gammon and ham cuts and cooking methods 83
Balancing your diet 249–50
Beef cuts and cooking methods 84–5

Calories, food and drink 219–28
Calorific yields of foods *see* Energy yields
Cheese, types 155–6
Chicken sizes 94
Coffee, storage times 192
Conversions:
  Liquid and dry measures:
    UK imperial to metric 21
    US customary to metric 21
  Liquid measures: metric to UK imperial 17
  Liquid measures: metric to US customary 19
  Liquid measures: UK imperial to metric 16
  Liquid measures: US customary to metric 18
  Oven temperatures 25
  UK cups and spoonfuls to UK imperial and metric 23
  UK imperial to US customary units 20
  US cups and spoonfuls to US customary and metric 23
  US customary to UK imperial units 20
  Weights: metric to UK imperial 15
  Weights: UK imperial to metric 14

Dairy products, storage times 158

E numbers *see* Additives
Egg sizes 153; and uses 154
Energy yields of foods 219

Fat composition of oils and other foods 199
Fish buying seasons: oily fish 110
Fish buying seasons: white fish 109
Fish, cooking methods and times 113–4
Fish, storage times 112
Fish, types 106–7
Freezers, food storage times 59
Fruit, freezing 135–6
Fruit, types 124–9
Fruit, when to buy 130

Game birds, roasting times 103
Game (furred), roasting times 104
Game, hanging times 97
Game, storage times 98
Game, thawing times 100
Gaming seasons 96
Gas oven shelf temperatures 50

Lamb cuts and cooking methods 85
Liquid and other volume measures: conversions 16–23

Meat, boiling times 93
Meat cuts and cooking methods:
  Bacon, gammon and ham cuts 83
  Beef cuts 84–5
  Lamb cuts 85
  Pork cuts 82
  Veal cuts 86
Meat, grilling and frying times 92

Meat, roasting times 90–1
Meat, storage times 88
Meat, thawing times 89
Milk equivalents 152
Minerals, major 210–13
Minerals, trace 214–17

Nuts, storage times 142
Nuts, types 140

Oils, fat composition 199
Oils, smoking temperatures 163

Pasta, types 164–6
Pork cuts and cooking methods 82
Poultry, roasting times 101–2
Poultry sizes *see* chicken sizes
Poultry, storage times 98
Poultry, thawing times 99
Pulses, minimum boiling times 143–4
Pulses, storage times 142
Pulses, types 141

Refrigerators, food storage times 57
Refrigerators, where to put food 55–6

Shellfish buying seasons 110–11
Shellfish, cooking methods and times 114
Shellfish, storage times 112
Shellfish, types 107
Sodium (salt) content of selected foods 209
Spoonful equivalents for ingredients 24
Storage times, freezer 59
Storage times, miscellaneous foods 173–5

Storage times, refrigerator 57

Tea, storage times 192
Temperature, oven, conversions 25

Veal cuts and cooking methods 86
Vegetables, boiling and steaming times 138–9
Vegetables, freezing 132–3
Vegetables, types 115–24
Vegetables, when to buy 131
Vitamins, fat-soluble 206–7
Vitamins, water-soluble 202–05
Volume measures: conversions 16–24

Weights: conversions 14–15
Wine quality classifications and terms:
  Austrian wine 178
  Bulgarian wine 178
  French wine 179
  German wine 180
  Italian wine 181
  North American wine (terms only) 182
  Portuguese wine 182
  Spanish wine 183
Wine, recommended serving temperatures 186

1. Weights and measures

This section includes an explanation of the systems of weights and volumes used to measure foods. There are also conversion tables for weight, volume and temperature measures. For practicality when cooking or shopping, the conversions given in the tables are approximate but sufficiently accurate to ensure success in most recipes. Exact conversions can be made using the formulae provided.

WEIGHT AND VOLUME MEASURES

Weights

Foods are sold in either metric or imperial weights. The metric or international system of units uses grams (g) and kilograms (kg). The imperial (Avoirdupois) system uses ounces (oz) and pounds (lb). Use the tables on pp. 14–15 to convert values from imperial to metric, and vice versa. Although the metric system has been officially adopted, the UK imperial system and the US customary system are still in everyday use.

> *Note:* UK imperial weight measures are equivalent to US customary weight measures; the tables on pp. 14–15 can be used for both.

Liquid measures

Bottled or packaged liquids are sold in metric or imperial volumes. The metric system uses litres (l) and millilitres (ml). The imperial system uses pints (pt) and fluid ounces (fl oz).

> *Note:* UK imperial and US customary liquid measures are different. Use the tables on pp. 16–17 to convert values from UK imperial to metric, and vice versa. Use the tables on pp. 18–19 to convert values from US customary to metric units, and vice versa. Use the formulae on p. 20 to convert between UK imperial and US customary volume measures.

Other volume measures

- On p. 20 you will find equivalent weights in metric and UK imperial units for volumes of water.
- The first table on p. 21 sets out a range of UK imperial units for liquid and dry volumes.

> *Note:* UK imperial liquid and dry volume measures are equivalent.

- The second table on p. 21 sets out a range of US customary units for liquid and dry volumes.

> *Note:* US customary liquid and dry volume measures are not equivalent.

- The tables on p. 23 give cup and spoon measures with their UK imperial, US customary and metric equivalents.
- The table on p. 24 gives spoonful equivalents for various common ingredients.

WEIGHTS

UK imperial to metric conversions

The imperial pound (lb) equals 16 ounces (oz), which is equal to 0.454 kilograms (kg) – slightly less than 1/2 kilogram (500 g).

1 lb or 16 oz	=	0.454 kg or 454 g
1/2 lb or 8 oz	=	0.227 kg or 227 g
1/4 lb or 4 oz	=	0.113 kg or 113 g
1 oz	=	28 g

UK imperial to metric
Approximate conversions for kitchen use

Imperial	Metric	Imperial	Metric
1 oz	30 g	13 oz	370 g
2 oz	60 g	14 oz	400 g
3 oz	85 g	15 oz	425 g
4 oz	110 g	(1 lb) 16 oz	450 g
5 oz	140 g	1 1/2 lb	680 g
6 oz	170 g	2 lb	910 g
7 oz	200 g	2 1/2 lb	1.1 kg
(1/2 lb) 8 oz	225 g	3 lb	1.4 kg
9 oz	255 g	3 1/2 lb	1.6 kg
10 oz	280 g	4 lb	1.8 kg
11 oz	310 g	4 1/2 lb	2 kg
12 oz	340 g	5 lb	2.3 kg

Accurate conversions

oz	→ g	x 28.349
lb	→ kg	x 0.454

Metric to UK imperial conversions

The metric kilogram (kg) equals 1000 grams (g), which is equal to 2.205 pounds (lb) – just over 35 ounces (oz).

1 kg or 1000 g	=	2.205 lb or 35.27 oz
1/2 kg or 500 g	=	1.102 lb or 17.63 oz
100 g	=	3.527 oz
10 g	=	0.353 oz

Metric to UK imperial
Approximate conversions for kitchen use

Metric	Imperial	Metric	Imperial
15 g	1/2 oz	910 g	2 lb
30 g	1 oz	1 kg	2 1/4 lb
60 g	2 oz	1.5 kg	3 1/4 lb
100 g	3 1/2 oz	2 kg	4 1/2 lb
200 g	7 oz	2.5 kg	5 1/2 lb
300 g	10 1/2 oz	3 kg	6 1/2 lb
400 g	14 oz	3.5 kg	7 3/4 lb
500 g	17 1/2 oz	4 kg	8 3/4 lb
600 g	21 oz	4.5 kg	10 lb
700 g	25 oz	5 kg	11 lb
800 g	28 oz		

Accurate conversions

g ⟶ oz	x 0.035
kg ⟶ lb	x 2.205

Note: UK imperial weight measures are equivalent to US customary weight measures.

LIQUID MEASURES

UK imperial to metric conversions

The imperial pint (pt) equals 20 fluid ounces (fl oz), which is equal to 0.568 litres (l) – slightly more than 1/2 litre (500 ml).

1 pt or 20 fl oz	=	0.568 l or 568 ml
3/4 pt or 15 fl oz	=	0.426 l or 426 ml
1/2 pt or 10 fl oz	=	0.284 l or 284 ml
1/4 pt or 5 fl oz	=	142 ml

UK imperial to metric
Approximate conversions for kitchen use

Imperial	Metric	Imperial	Metric
1 fl oz	30 ml	9 fl oz	255 ml
2 fl oz	60 ml	(1/2 pt) 10 fl oz	280 ml
3 fl oz	85 ml	(3/4 pt) 15 fl oz	425 ml
4 fl oz	110 ml	(1 pt) 20 fl oz	570 ml
(1/4 pt) 5 fl oz	140 ml	(1 qrt) 2 pt	1.1 l
6 fl oz	170 ml	3 pt	1.7 l
7 fl oz	200 ml	4 pt	2.3 l
8 fl oz	225 ml	(1 gal) 8 pt	4.5 l

Accurate conversions

pt (UK) →	l	x 0.568
fl oz (UK) →	ml	x 28.4

Metric to UK imperial conversions

The metric litre (l) equals 1000 millilitres (ml), which is equal to 1.76 pints (pt) – just over 35 fluid ounces (fl oz).

1 l or 100 cl or 1000 ml	=	1.76 pt or 35.2 fl oz
1/2 l or 50 cl or 500 ml	=	0.88 pt or 17.6 fl oz
10 cl or 100 ml	=	3.52 fl oz
1 cl or 10 ml	=	0.352 fl oz

Metric to UK imperial
Approximate conversions for kitchen use

Metric	Imperial	Metric	Imperial
15 ml	1/2 fl oz	900 ml	31 1/2 fl oz
30 ml	1 fl oz	1 l	35 fl oz
60 ml	2 fl oz	1.5 l	2 3/4 pt
100 ml	3 1/2 fl oz	2 l	3 1/2 pt
200 ml	7 fl oz	2.5 l	4 1/2 pt
300 ml	10 1/2 fl oz	3 l	5 1/4 pt
400 ml	14 fl oz	3.5 l	6 1/4 pt
500 ml	17 1/2 fl oz	4 l	7 pt
600 ml	21 fl oz	4.5 l	8 pt
700 ml	24 1/2 fl oz	5 l	8 3/4 pt
800 ml	28 fl oz		

Accurate conversions

l	→ pt (UK)	x 1.76
ml	→ fl oz (UK)	x 0.035

US customary to metric conversions

The customary pint (pt) equals 16 fluid ounces (fl oz), which is equal to 0.473 litres (l) – slightly less than 1/2 litre (500 ml).

1 pt or 16 fl oz	=	0.473 l or 473 ml
3/4 pt or 12 fl oz	=	0.355 l or 355 ml
1/2 pt or 8 fl oz	=	0.237 l or 237 ml
1/4 pt or 4 fl oz	=	118 ml

US customary to metric
Approximate conversions for kitchen use

Customary	Metric	Customary	Metric
1 fl oz	30 ml	11 fl oz	330 ml
2 fl oz	60 ml	(3/4 pt) 12 fl oz	360 ml
3 fl oz	90 ml	13 fl oz	390 ml
(1/4 pt) 4 fl oz	120 ml	14 fl oz	420 ml
5 fl oz	150 ml	15 fl oz	450 ml
6 fl oz	180 ml	(1 pt) 16 fl oz	480 ml
7 fl oz	210 ml	(1 qt) 2 pt	950 ml
(1/2 pt) 8 fl oz	240 ml	3 pt	1.4 l
9 fl oz	270 ml	4 pt	1.9 l
10 fl oz	300 ml	(1 gal) 8 pt	3.8 l

Accurate conversions

pt (US)	→ l	x 0.473
fl oz (US)	→ ml	x 29.57

Metric to US customary conversions

The metric litre (l) equals 1000 millilitres (ml), which is equal to 2.113 customary pints (pt) – just under 34 fluid ounces (fl oz).

1 l or 100 cl or 1000 ml	=	2.113 pt or 33.81 fl oz
$^1/_2$ l or 50 cl or 500 ml	=	1.056 pt or 16.9 fl oz
10 cl or 100 ml	=	3.381 fl oz
1 cl or 10 ml	=	0.338 fl oz

Metric to US customary
Approximate conversions for kitchen use

Metric	Customary	Metric	Customary
10 ml	$^1/_3$ fl oz	900 ml	30 fl oz
25 ml	1 fl oz	(1 l) 1000 ml	2 pt
50 ml	$1^2/_3$ fl oz	1.5 l	$3^1/_4$ pt
100 ml	$3^1/_2$ fl oz	2 l	$4^1/_4$ pt
200 ml	7 fl oz	2.5 l	$5^1/_4$ pt
300 ml	10 fl oz	3 l	$6^1/_4$ pt
400 ml	$13^1/_2$ fl oz	3.5 l	$7^1/_2$ pt
($^1/_2$ l) 500 ml	17 fl oz	4 l	$8^1/_2$ pt
600 ml	20 fl oz	4.5 l	$9^1/_2$ pt
700 ml	23 fl oz	5 l	$10^1/_2$ pt
800 ml	27 fl oz		

Accurate conversions

l	→ pt (US)	x 2.113
ml	→ fl oz (US)	x 0.034

UK imperial to US customary conversions

The UK imperial pint (pt) equals 20 fluid ounces (fl oz), which is equal to 1.201 US customary pints (pt).

Accurate conversions

fl oz (UK) →	fl oz (US)	x 0.961
pt (UK) →	pt (US)	x 1.201

US customary to UK imperial conversions

The US customary pint (pt) equals 16 fluid ounces (fl oz), which is equal to 0.833 UK imperial pints (pt).

Accurate conversions

fl oz (US) →	fl oz (UK)	x 1.041
pt (US) →	pt (UK)	x 0.833

OTHER VOLUME MEASURES

Water weights

Below you will find equivalent water volumes for UK imperial and metric weights.

Water volume		Weight
1 fluid ounce (fl oz)	=	1 ounce (oz)
1 pint (pt)/20 fl oz	=	$1^1/_4$ pounds (lb)/20 oz
1 millilitre (ml)	=	1 gram (g)
1 litre (l)	=	1 kilogram (kg)

UK imperial liquid and dry measures

1 bushel (bu)	=	4 pecks (pk)	=	36.35 l
1 peck (pk)	=	2 gallons (gal)	=	9.09 l
1 gallon (gal)	=	4 quarts (qrt)	=	4.55 l
1 quart (qrt)	=	2 pints (pt)	=	1.14 l
1 pint (pt)	=	4 gills (gi)	=	568 ml
1 gill (gi)	=	5 fluid ounces (fl oz)	=	142 ml
1 fluid ounce (fl oz)	=	8 fluid drams (fl dr)	=	28.41 ml
1 fluid dram (fl dr)	=	60 minims (min) or 60 drops	=	3.55 ml
1 minim (min)	=	1 drop	=	0.06 ml

US customary liquid and dry measures

Liquid

1 gallon (gal)	=	4 quarts (qt)	=	3.78 l
1 quart (qt)	=	2 pints (pt)	=	0.95 l
1 pint (pt)	=	4 gills (gi)	=	0.47 l
1 gill (gi)	=	4 fluid ounces (fl oz)	=	118.3 ml
1 fluid ounce (fl oz)	=	8 fluid drams (fl dr)	=	29.6 ml
1 fluid dram (fl dr)	=	60 minims (min) or 60 drops	=	3.7 ml
1 minim (min)	=	1 drop	=	0.06 ml

Dry

1 bushel (bu)	=	4 pecks (pk)	=	35.24 l
1 peck (pk)	=	8 quarts (qt)	=	8.81 l
1 quart (qt)	=	2 pints (pt)	=	1.1 l
1 pint (pt)	=	1/2 quart (qt)	=	0.55 l

Cups and spoonfuls

Note: US cup measures are not equal to UK cup measures. For conversion, 1 British cup is equal to $1\frac{1}{4}$ US cups.

Measuring with cups and spoons

Standard cup and spoon measures in recipes usually refer to level measures. To achieve a level measure:

- For 'dry' ingredients, fill the cup or spoon and level it off with the back of a knife. If the ingredients are lumpy, sift them before you measure them.
- For liquids, always scrape out the cup or spoon to get the full measure. A rubber scraper or spatula is a useful tool for this.
- Fats are measured more easily at room temperature, when they are soft; do not try to measure fats directly from the fridge. Again, make sure you get the full measure by scraping out the measuring cup or spoon.

Levelling a teaspoon or tablespoon with a knife

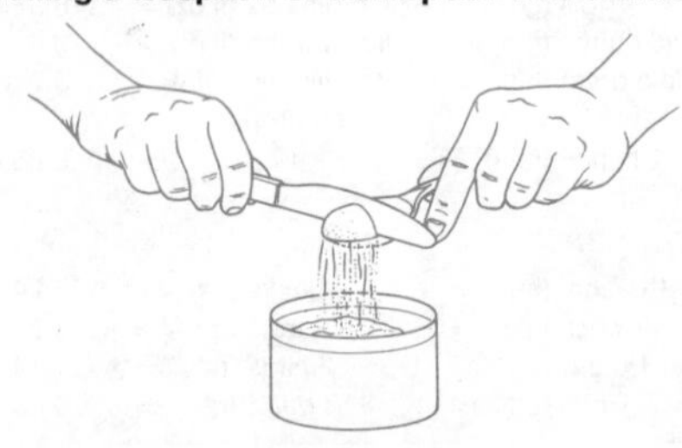

Cup and spoonful equivalents

The following tables give cup and spoonful measures with UK imperial, US customary and metric unit equivalents.

UK cups and spoonfuls

Cups/spoonfuls		UK imperial		Metric
2 cups	=	1 pint	=	568 ml
1 cup	=	10 fl oz	=	284 ml
1/2 cup	=	1 gill or 5 fl oz	=	142 ml
	=	10 tablespoons		
1 tablespoon	=	1/2 fl oz	=	15 ml
	=	3 teaspoons		
1 teaspoon	=	1/6 fl oz	=	5 ml

US cups and spoonfuls

Cups/spoonfuls		US customary		Metric
2 cups	=	1 pint	=	475 ml
1 cup	=	8 fl oz	=	237 ml
1/2 cup	=	1 gill or 4 fl oz	=	119 ml
	=	8 tablespoons		
1 tablespoon	=	1/2 fl oz	=	15 ml
	=	3 teaspoons		
1 teaspoon	=	1/6 fl oz	=	5 ml

Spoonful equivalents for ingredients
The table below gives the number of level tablespoons needed to measure approximately 30 g or 1 oz of various ingredients.

Common ingredients measured in spoonfuls

Tablespoons (tbsp) needed for 30 g or 1 oz (UK imperial/US customary) of an ingredient

Breadcrumbs	dried	3 tbsp
	fresh	7 tbsp
Butter		2 tbsp
Cheese	(grated cheddar)	3 tbsp
	(grated parmesan)	4 tbsp
Cocoa		4 tbsp
Coffee	ground	4 1/2 tbsp
	instant	6 1/2 tbsp
Cornflour		2 3/4 tbsp
Custard powder		2 3/4 tbsp
Flour	(unsifted)	3 tbsp
Gelatine	(powdered)	3 tbsp
Honey		1 tbsp
Lard		2 tbsp
Margarine		2 tbsp
Milk	(powdered, dried, skimmed)	5 tbsp
Parsley	(freshly chopped)	10 tbsp
Rice	uncooked	2 tbsp
Suet	shredded	3 tbsp
Sugar	(caster, demerara, granulated)	2 tbsp
Sugar	icing	3 tbsp
Syrup		1 tbsp
Yeast (dried)		2 tbsp

TEMPERATURE MEASURES

On electric cookers the oven temperatures are given in Celsius (°C) or Fahrenheit (°F). On gas cookers the oven temperature is shown in gas marks (regulo). For temperature conversions use the formulae and table below.

°F ⟶ °C Subtract 32, divide by 9 and then multiply by 5.
°C ⟶ °F Multiply by 9, divide by 5 and then add 32.

Oven temperatures

°F	°C	Gas mark	Temperature
225	110	1/4	Slow cooking
250	120	1/2	Very cool
275	140	1	Very cool
300	150	2	Cool
325	160	3	Warm
350	180	4	Moderate
375	190	5	Fairly hot
400	200	6	Fairly hot
425	220	7	Hot
450	230	8	Very hot
475	250	9	Very hot

Note: Fan-assisted ovens cook more efficiently than ordinary electric ovens. As a guide, for fan-assisted ovens reduce the temperature by 20 °C (68 °F). For more information about how to cook with different ovens *see* pp. 48–53 in **Section 3, Equipment and Utensils**.

2. Glossaries

The first glossary in this section defines cooking methods. The second covers unusual ingredients from a wide range of international cuisines, together with alternative food names which you may come across in recipe books. For full lists of food types (e.g. kinds of pasta, rice, etc.) see **Section 4**, **Food** (pp. 81–192).

COOKING METHODS AND PROCESSES

acidulate To make food slightly acid (e.g. by adding lemon juice or vinegar).

agitate To gently shake the contents of a pan.

à la paysanne

à la paysanne To cut into thin, even pieces that are round, square or triangular.

al dente Pasta which has been cooked so that it is just firm to the bite.

amandine To cook or coat with almonds.

arroser To sprinkle with a liquid, or to baste.

assaisonner To season.

bain-marie A form of poaching in which food is placed in a container which is in turn placed into another container (the bain-marie) half full

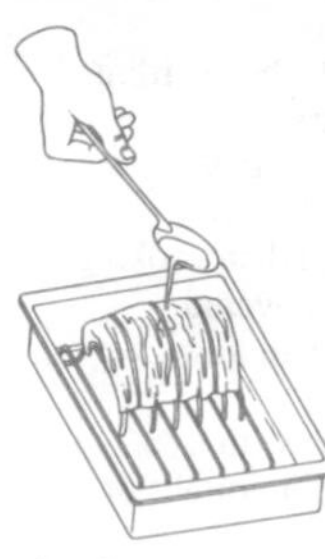
baste

beat

with heated water.
bake To cook in an oven or oven-like appliance.
bake blind To line a tart tin with pastry and bake it before adding the filling.
barbecue To roast slowly over burning coals or under a heat source on a rack or spit.
bard To tie slices of fatty bacon over the breast of poultry or game.
baste To moisten food with the fatty liquid in which it is cooking.
bat out To flatten raw meat slices with a cutlet bat.
beat To make a mixture smooth and aerated by rapidly turning it using a hand beater, electric mixer, wire whisk or spoon.
bind (1) To add eggs, melted fat or cream to stick dry ingredients together. (2) To add starch to a liquid to solidify or thicken it.
blanch To plunge food briefly into boiling water and then immediately into cold water.
blend To combine ingredients with a spoon, beater or electric blender until a uniform mixture is achieved.
boil To cook in water at 100 °C (212 °F). At this temperature water

bubbles rapidly.

bone To remove the bones from fish, meat or poultry.

braise

braise To cook meat and/or vegetables by first lightly browning in fat and then cooking slowly in a tightly covered container with a small quantity of water.

bread To coat food with breadcrumbs, biscuit crumbs or cereal crumbs.

broil The US and Canadian term for grilling, i.e. to cook food uncovered directly under heat or over an open fire.

brown To make food turn brown on the surface, usually by cooking at a high temperature in a little fat.

brush To spread fat, milk or beaten egg onto the surface of food, using a pastry brush.

chop

caramelize To heat sugar or foods containing sugar until the sugar melts and turns brown.

casserole To cook meat, seafood or poultry with vegetables in the oven in a casserole dish.

chine To separate the backbone from the ribs in a joint of meat.

chop To cut into small pieces.

clarify To make fats clear and free

of impurities by heating and draining through a fine filter.

coat a spoon To test the thickness of a sauce: if a spoon dipped into a sauce emerges with a thick, even coating, the consistency is right.

cream

coddle To simmer food in water just below boiling point.

cool (1) To leave food to stand at room temperature until it is no longer warm to the touch. (2) To refrigerate.

cream To beat a mixture with a spoon or mixer until it is the consistency of cream.

crimp (1) To gash or score meat with a knife. (2) To make a decorative border on a pie crust.

crimp

curdle To cause a sauce or fresh milk to separate into liquid and solids by overheating.

cure To preserve meat or fish by salting, drying or smoking.

cut in To combine flour and fat or other dry ingredients with a cutting motion, using two knives, until the fat is broken up and coated with flour.

decant (1) To gently pour off a liquid without stirring up any sediment at the bottom. (2) To pour a liquid from one bottle

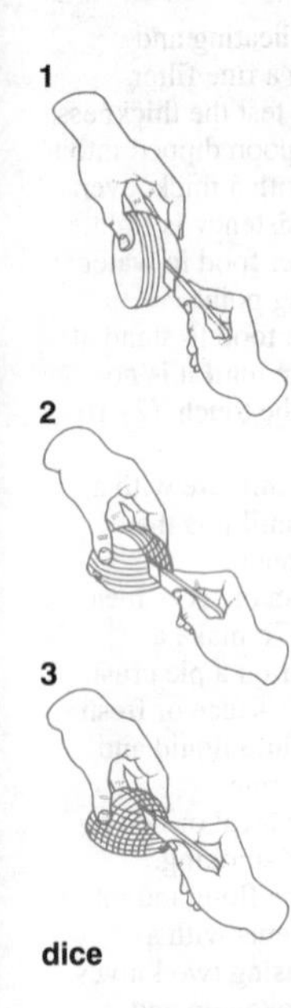

dice

to another.
deep-fry To fry food by immersing it completely in hot oil.
déglacer To make a sauce or gravy from the juices and food fragments remaining in the bottom of a pan.
dégraisser To skim fat off a liquid.
devil To coat food with a mixture of highly seasoned ingredients (e.g. mustard or hot spices).
dice To cut into small cubes.
dilute (1) To mix a powder, e.g. flour, with a liquid. (2) To add water to a concentrated liquid.
dot To sprinkle with small pieces of an ingredient, usually fat.
dredge To cover with a sprinkling of flour or sugar.
dress (1) To mix a salad with a sauce or dressing. (2) To remove the head, tail, fins, scales and insides of a fish before cooking. (3) To pluck, draw and truss poultry or game.
dust To sprinkle lightly with flour or sugar.
en papillotte To cook food in tightly sealed, oiled grease-proof paper or foil so that no steam escapes.
fillet To remove the bones and fat from meat, poultry or fish.

flake To break into natural segments.
flambé *see* **flame**.
flame To ignite spirits poured over a dish (as with Christmas pudding).
flour To coat with seasoned flour, usually before frying.
flute To make a decorative indented edging, e.g. around a piecrust.

fold

fold To combine one ingredient or mixture with another by turning them gently with a spatula or metal spoon.
frost To cover a cake with a thin layer of icing sugar.
fry To cook food in fat or oil over direct heat.
garnish To enhance a dish with edible decorations.
glaze To coat food with a shiny liquid finish, e.g. a sauce or syrup.
grate To shred food by rubbing it against a grater.
grease To coat the inside of a pan or dish with fat.
grill To cook uncovered food directly under heat or over an open fire.

frost

hang To suspend game in a dry, cool place to allow time for enzymes to tenderize and improve the flavour of the flesh.

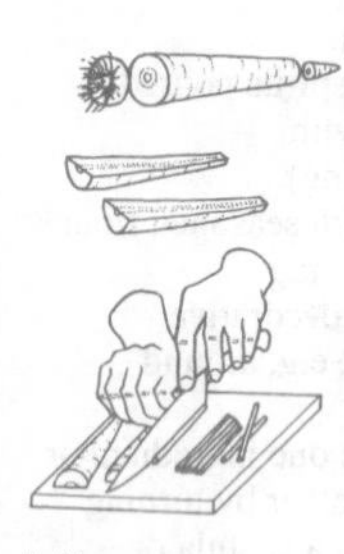

julienne

hull To remove the leaves and stems from soft fruit.
infuse To flavour a liquid by soaking herbs, leaves or other ingredients in it.
joint To divide game, meat or poultry into pieces.
julienne To cut vegetables into fine strips.
knead To stretch, press and fold dough or a similar mixture until it has a smooth texture.
knock up To encourage flaky pastry layers to separate during cooking by making small cuts in the edges.

knead

lard To thread thin strips of fat through meat which is too lean.
leaven To use an ingredient such as yeast, baking powder or eggs to make other ingredients rise in cooking.
line To place greaseproof paper inside a cooking tin.
macerate To soak food in a liquid.
marinate To tenderize and flavour food before cooking by soaking it in a seasoned liquid.
microwave To cook or reheat food in a microwave oven.

mix

mix To combine ingredients by continuous stirring.
mouler To grind dry food into a powder or soft food into a purée.
oil a mould To brush oil over the insides of a container to prevent food from sticking to it.
parblanch Removing salt or strong tastes from food by boiling it for a short time and then plunging it into cold water.
parboil To boil until partially cooked.
pare To peel the skin from a food.
pass To pass ingredients through a strainer or sieve.
pasteurize To kill microorganisms in milk by heating.
peel To take the skin off something, usually a fruit or vegetable.
pickle To preserve meat or vegetables in a vinegar or salt solution.
pipe To decorate by applying icing, purée, butter, etc. through a forcing bag and nozzle.
pluck To remove the feathers from poultry or a game bird.
poach To cook food very gently in a simmering liquid, just below boiling point.

pipe

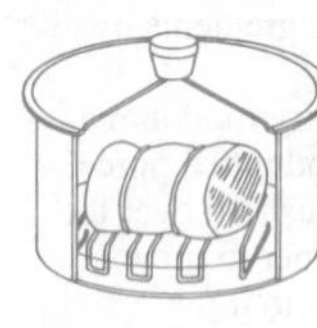
pot roast

pot roast (pôelé) To cook large cuts of meat by browning in fat and then cooking slowly in a covered pot.
preheat To set an oven at the desired cooking temperature some time before it is needed so that the food to be cooked is placed into an oven that is already hot.
preserve To treat food so that it keeps in good condition.
pressure cook To cook food using steam under pressure in a special sealable pot.
prove To allow a yeast dough to rise and expand by leaving it to rest in a warm place.
pulp To reduce food to a soft mass by boiling or crushing.
purée To sieve, mash or liquidize food into a smooth, thick paste.
raise To use an ingredient such as yeast, baking powder or eggs to make other ingredients rise in cooking.
réchauffer To reheat.
reconstitute To restore concentrated food to its original state by adding water.
reduce To concentrate a liquid by boiling it without a cover, causing water to evaporate.

rub

rehydrate To soak dried foods so that they reabsorb water.
relax To let pastry stand, especially after rolling out, so that it is not stretched.
rest To let batter stand for half an hour to allow starch grains to swell before cooking.
rissoler To fry to a golden brown.
roast To cook food in heated air, usually in an oven.
rub To rub fat and flour together with the fingers until the mixture resembles breadcrumbs.
sauté To cook food rapidly in a frying pan using a small amount of fat, until it turns golden-brown.

sauté

scald (1) To pour boiling water over something. (2) To heat milk until it begins to bubble and rise.
scallop To alternate solid food with layers of creamy sauce.
score To make a series of shallow cuts on the surface of food.
seal To seal the outside surface of meat by heating it quickly in an oven or pan so that colour and juices are retained.
sear To brown the surface of food by cooking over direct heat or in the oven at high temperature.
season To improve flavour by

adding salt, pepper, spices or herbs.

shallow-fry To fry food using just enough preheated fat to stop the food sticking to the pan.

shell To remove nuts from their shells, or peas from their pods.

shred To cut food into slithers.

sift To remove lumps from or thoroughly mix ingredients by passing them through a sieve.

skim

simmer To cook food gently just below boiling point, at around 85–93 °C (185–200 °F).

singe To brown or colour by applying heat to the surface.

skewer To fasten food onto a pointed wooden or metal stick.

skim To remove fat or scum from the surface of a liquid.

skin To remove the skin from food.

skin

slake To mix cornflower or a similar ingredient with a cold liquid to make a thin paste before adding a hot liquid to cook the starch.

souse To pickle food in vinegar or salt water.

steam To cook food in steam (moist heat).

sterilize To destroy dangerous

strain

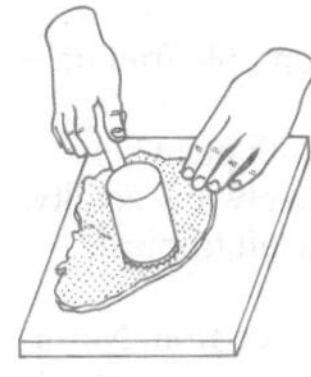
tenderize

organisms by heat.

stew To simmer food gently, usually in the oven.

stir To mix something gently, using circular motions with a spoon.

stir-fry To cook small pieces of food in a wok over high heat.

strain To separate solids from liquids using a sieve or muslin.

sweat To cook vegetables very slowly in butter or oil.

tenderize To make meat more tender by beating with a meat mallet or by adding certain herbs, spices and juices.

toast To brown food in a dry heat.

toss (1) To turn over the contents of a pan by throwing the food lightly upwards. (2) To use utensils to lift and turn a salad, mixing it with a dressing in the process.

truss To secure poultry with string and/or skewers so that it will hold its shape during cooking.

whip To beat very rapidly, using a hand or electric whisk, until the liquid becomes foamy.

whisk To beat air into eggs, cream or batter using a looped wire utensil (a whisk).

COOKING INGREDIENTS

agar-agar A vegetarian gelatine, made from seaweed.
alfalfa A plant with tiny seeds which are sprouted and used in salads or casseroles.
allumettes Vegetables cut into thin strips.
anaheim (Californian green chilli) A mild-tasting chilli with bright green pod, 12–18 cm (5–7 in) long. Used in Mexican cooking.
arrowroot A fine-grained starch prepared from the rhizomes of a tropical plant. Excellent for thickening sauces.
arugula *See* **rocket**.
asafetida A pungent brown resin used in Indian cooking.
aubergine The large, egg-shaped dark purple fruit of the eggplant.
balsamic vinegar Vinegar flavoured with plant extracts. Has a sweet flavour and relatively low acidity.
bamboo shoots The young shoots of a tall tropical grass. Used in Oriental cooking.
basmati rice A fine-grained, aromatic rice from North India and Pakistan.
bean curd Milky, white, custard-like squares made from soaked, mashed and strained soya beans. Used in Asian cooking.
beans *See* **Section 4, Food** (p. 141), for a full list of varieties of beans, peas and lentils.
bean sauce A fine or coarse purée of fermented soya beans. Used in Oriental cooking.
benne oil The Malaysian term for sesame oil.
bhindi (lady's finger/okra) Oblong sticky green

vegetable pod used in Indian cooking.
bitter gourd A courgette-shaped vegetable of the marrow family. Used in Asian cooking.
black salt Dark, pungent salt used in Indian cooking.
blini A Russian pancake made of buckwheat and yeast.
bottarga The dried and salted roe (eggs) of mullet and tuna. Used in Italian cooking.
bouillon The unclarified stock or broth from fish, meat or vegetables.
bouquet garni A bunch of herbs, including marjoram, thyme and parsley. Used to flavour stews and soups.
bread *See* **Section 4, Food** (p. 159), for a full list of varieties of breads.
brioche A slightly sweet, soft bread roll made from a light yeast dough.
bulgar wheat Cracked kernels of boiled and dried wheat. Used in Middle Eastern cooking.
Californian green chilli *See* **anaheim**.
cantaloupe A variety of melon with a ribbed rind and orange flesh.
capers The buds of a Mediterranean shrub. Used pickled in sauces and garnishes.
carambola (star fruit) A yellow fruit from an Indonesian tree. Used to decorate fruit salads and ice cream.
carob flour A chocolate-like powder prepared by grinding the ripe dried pod of the carob tree. Used in cakes and biscuits or to make drinks, desserts and sweets.
cassava (tapioca) A root vegetable resembling a large, brown sweet potato.
caviar The salted roe (eggs) of sturgeon.

cayenne pepper A hot condiment, made from the dried red seeds and pods of a tropical plant.
celeriac A type of celery with a large turnip-like root.
chantilly Slightly sweetened whipped cream, sometimes flavoured with vanilla.
chapati flour Finely ground wholewheat flour, usually made from wheat that is low in gluten. Used to make many kinds of Indian breads.
chard (Swiss chard) A variety of beet with succulent leaves and thick stalks.
cheese *See* **Section 4**, **Food** (pp. 155–6), for more information on types of cheese.
chiffonade A garnish of shredded lettuce, spinach and sorrel.
Chinese peas *See* snow peas.
chorizo A highly seasoned, smoked pork sausage used in Spanish and Mexican cooking.
choux pastry Light pastry made by beating eggs into a cooked paste of flour, fat and water.
clotted cream A very thick cream which can be spread.
coquille The French term for scallop.
corn starch The US and Canadian term for cornflour.
cotechino A variety of Italian spiced pork sausage.
coulis A concentrated liquid, usually from fish or meat, obtained by long slow cooking.
crème fraîche Matured, lightly fermented cream which has not been allowed to go sour.
crêpe A thin pancake.
croûtons Small cubes or other shapes of bread, deep-fried until golden and used as a garnish.
curd A semi-solid substance formed by the coagulation of milk.

dashi A clear stock made from tuna and seaweed. Used in Japanese cooking.
doong gwooh A Chinese dried mushroom, brownish-black in colour, with a stronger and more distinctive flavour than fresh mushrooms.
dripping The fat that exudes from meat, poultry or game during roasting.
dumpling A small ball of dough, usually cooked and served with stew.
duxelle A purée of finely chopped mushrooms, cooked in butter with chopped shallots. Used for stuffing meat or as a basis for sauces.
eggplant *See* **aubergine**.
endive A lettuce-like vegetable, the frilly leaves of which are used in salads.
escalopes Thin slices of meat, usually veal, which are beaten flat and shallow fried.
farina Fine flour made from wheat, potatoes and nuts.
felafel Ground chickpeas shaped into balls and deep fried. Used in eastern Mediterranean dishes.
filo pastry Made from paper-thin sheets of pastry dough.
fines herbes A mixture of finely chopped chervil, chives, parsley and tarragon.
foie gras The preserved livers of specially fattened ducks or geese.
fumet The concentrated liquid in which fish, meat or vegetables has been cooked.
galanga root A root of the ginger family. Used in Southeast Asian cooking.
garam masala A mixture of spices, including cinnamon, cardamom and cloves. Hot to the taste and

used in Indian cooking.
garbanzos The Spanish and Mexican term for chickpeas.
gelatine A solid protein made by boiling animal bones and hides. Used to make jellies and other gelatinous foods.
ghee Butter which has been clarified by boiling and is totally free of milk solids. It has a nutty flavour and is used in Indian dishes.
giblets The edible internal organs and trimmings of poultry and game, including the gizzard, liver, heart and neck.
ginseng A Korean root used in salads, for flavouring and to make ginseng tea.
glace de viande A concentrated meat stock.
gnocchi Dumplings made from semolina paste, potatoes or choux pastry.
grappa An Italian spirit made from the remains of grapes after they have been used for wine making.
gravlax A dry-cured salmon, marinated in sugar, salt and spices. Used in Scandinavian cuisine.
grissini Breadsticks.
guava A tropical edible fruit, which turns from green to yellow when ripe. The fruit is best stewed or made into jam or jelly.
herbs *See* **Section 4, Food** (pp. 144–50), for a full list of herbs and spices.
hoisin sauce A thick red sauce that is sweet in flavour. Used in Chinese cooking with shellfish, spareribs, duck and vegetables.
icing A sweet coating used to decorate cakes, etc.
jalapeño A very hot, dark green chilli, about 5 cm

(2 in) long. Used in Mexican cooking.
jus The French term for the juice from roasting meat.
lady's finger *See* **bhindi**.
lard Natural or refined fat from a pig.
leaven A raising agent, such as yeast, that causes dough or batter to rise.
legumes Vegetables, especially beans or peas.
lemon grass A tall, greyish-green grass used for its aroma and flavour in Southeast Asian cooking. Gives a lemon-peel-like flavour.
luganega A lightly spiced variety of Italian pork sausage.
lychee A tropical fruit with a translucent flesh in a papery skin.
mangetout A variety of pea in which the vegetable pod is also edible. Includes **snow peas** and **sugar snap peas**.
mango An Asian fruit with sweet orange flesh.
maple syrup The concentrated sweet sap of the sugar maple and black maple, used to make sweets, puddings and as a sweetener on pancakes.
marinade A seasoned blend of oil, wine or vinegar in which food is soaked before cooking.
marsala A fortified wine used in Italian cooking.
mascarpone A thick Italian cream cheese made from cow's milk and used in sweet and savoury dishes.
medallions Small circular cuts of fish, meat or pâté.
mirabelle A small yellow plum, used as a tart filling.
mirin A thick sweet Japanese wine used for cooking.
miso A variety of pastes made from fermented soya beans and grains. Used as a flavouring in Japanese cooking.

molasses A by-product of sugar refining that can be used as a spread or in a similar way to golden syrup in recipes.
moules The French term for mussels.
noodles Flat ribbons of pasta.
nori The Japanese term for seaweed.
nuts *See* **Section 4**, **Foods** (p. 140), for a full list of varieties of nuts.
oil *See* **Section 4**, **Foods** (pp. 161–3), for a full list of varieties of oils.
okra *See* **bhindi**.
panada A mixture of flour and water or of bread soaked in milk, used to bind ingredients and as a thickening agent. Used in Spanish and South American cooking.
pancetta A mild, unsmoked Italian bacon.
papaya (pawpaw) A Caribbean fruit with sweet yellow flesh and small black seeds.
pasta *See* **Section 4**, **Food** (pp. 164–6), for a full list of pasta varieties.
pearl barley Barley which has been ground into small round grains. Used in soups and stews.
pectin A substance extracted from ripe fruit and vegetables which is used to set jams and jellies.
pesto A pasta sauce made with oil, parmesan cheese, garlic, nuts and basil leaves.
petit pois Tiny sweet green peas.
pignoli The Italian term for pine nuts.
pimiento A small red mild Spanish pepper, used in salads or as a stuffing for green olives.
pine nuts Seeds from Mediterranean pine cones, with a delicate nutty flavour. Used in Italian, Spanish and

Middle Eastern dishes. Also known as pine kernels.
pith In citrus fruit, the soft fibrous tissue lining the inside of the rind.
poblano A hot, dark green chilli of triangular shape and about 11 cm (4 in) long. Used in Mexican dishes.
porcini A fungus used in Italian cooking. It is usually dried.
prosciutto The Italian term for ham. There are several regional varieties (e.g. Prosciutto di Parma, which is known in English as Parma Ham).
pulp The fleshy tissue of fruits and vegetables.
pulses *See* **Section 4, Food** (p. 141), for a full list of pulses.
purée Raw or cooked food forced through a sieve or processed in an electric liquidizer.
ratafia A flavouring made from bitter almonds.
relish A spicy sauce made with fruit or vegetables.
rennet A substance containing the enzyme renin, extracted from the stomach lining of calves and used to coagulate milk for making cheese.
rice *See* **Section 4, Food** (pp. 167–8), for a full list of types of rice.
rocket (arugula) A peppery salad leaf plant widely used in Italian cooking.
roux A mixture of equal parts of flour and melted butter. Used as a base for savoury sauces.
sake Japanese rice wine.
salami A highly seasoned Italian pork sausage.
sauerkraut Shredded and pickled cabbage. Used in German cuisine.
scallion A collective term for salad vegetables with small root bulbs and long leaves, e.g. the spring onion.

scaloppine Small escalopes of veal, about 7.6 cm (3 in) square and weighing 28–43 g (1–1½ oz).
seasoned flour Flour flavoured with salt and pepper.
seasoning Salt, pepper, herbs or spices added to food to enhance flavour.
sesame oil An aromatic oil, particularly the unrefined, thick brownish version, made from sesame seeds. Used more as a flavouring than as a cooking oil.
shallot A vegetable similar to the onion.
shiitake A Japanese mushroom.
snow peas (Chinese peas) Very small peas in flat pea pods, eaten pod and all (known as mangetout peas).
soya beans Round, dull-yellow beans, used to make soya milk and bean curd, and which may be boiled or fried. Available in dried form.
soy sauce Sauces made from fermented soya beans, ranging in flavour from light to salty to syrupy-sweet.
spices *See* **Section 4, Foods** (pp. 144–50), for a full list of spices and herbs.
squash The US and Canadian term for a family of marrow-like vegetables.
starch Carbohydrate from cereals and potatoes.
star fruit *See* carambola.
suet The fat around beef and lamb kidneys and loins.
sugar snap peas Similar to **snow peas** but plumper. Eaten whole (known as mangetout peas).
sweeteners *See* **Section 4, Foods** (pp. 169–71), for a full list of sweeteners.
Swiss chard *See* **chard**.
taco A filled **tortilla**, usually fried.
tahini A paste made from sesame seeds. Used in Middle Eastern sauces and dips.

tapioca *See* **cassava.**
tofu Unfermented soya bean curd, made from soya bean milk.
tortilla A form of flat unleavened bread, originating in Mexico.
truffle A rare European mushroom-like fungus, black or white in colour. Regarded as a delicacy.
tutti-frutti Small pieces of candied mixed fruits, fresh or dried, added to ice-cream.
unleavened bread Bread which is made without a raising agent.
vanilla sugar Sugar flavoured with vanilla.
vinaigrette A salad dressing made from oil, vinegar, salt and pepper, and sometimes flavoured with herbs.
vinegar A clear, sour-tasting liquid, consisting of impure dilute acetic acid, made by the fermentation of wine, cider or malt beer.
water chestnut A dark, chestnut-sized bulb, grown in water. Used in Oriental cooking.
whey The liquid that separates from the curd when milk is coagulated for cheese-making.
yam A root of tropical climbing plants and a staple food in parts of Africa.
yeast Fungus cells used in raising dough for bread and for fermenting alcohol.
yoghurt A thick custard-like food, prepared by curdling milk using bacteria; often sweetened and flavoured with fruit or used plain in savoury dishes.
zest The grated rind of citrus fruits.
zucchini The US, Canadian and Italian term for courgette.

3. Equipment and utensils

This section describes a range of kitchen equipment and utensils, and gives some tips on usage. Items are grouped under the following headings: *cookers*, *refrigerators*, *freezers*, *food processing machines*, *measuring and weighing equipment*, *pots and pans*, *knives and other cutting tools*, *bakeware and moulds*, and *other hand tools*.

COOKERS

Electric cookers

In a standard electric oven the top shelf position is usually slightly hotter than the bottom. In fan-assisted electric ovens the temperature is uniform throughout, ensuring that food is cooked evenly and at the right temperature anywhere in the oven.

Positioning single dishes in an electric oven Currents of hot air rise faster through narrow spaces. In diagram **1** (*right*), food on side **a** of the dish will cook faster than food on side **b** because of the faster hot air current passing over it. To avoid uneven cooking, single dishes should be placed in the centre of the oven.

Positioning more than one dish in an electric oven Hot air needs to circulate all around a dish if it is to be cooked properly. In diagram **2** (*right*), the flow of air to the top of dish **c** and the bottom of dish **d** is interrupted. To avoid uneven cooking, dishes should be staggered as in diagram **3** and turned at intervals.

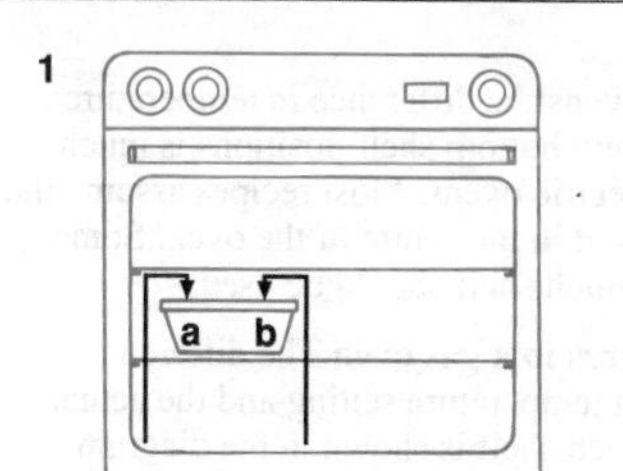
1
a
b

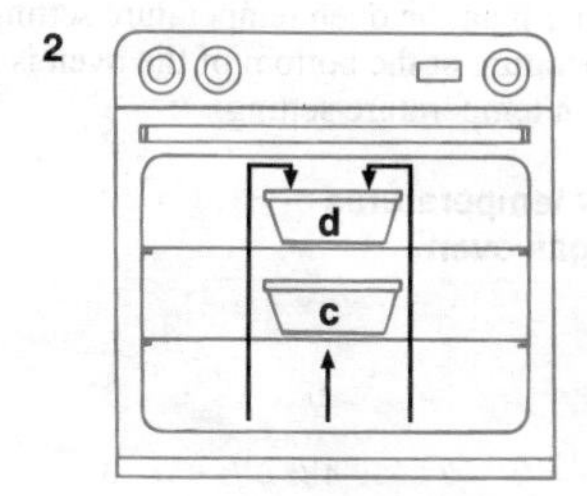
2
d
c

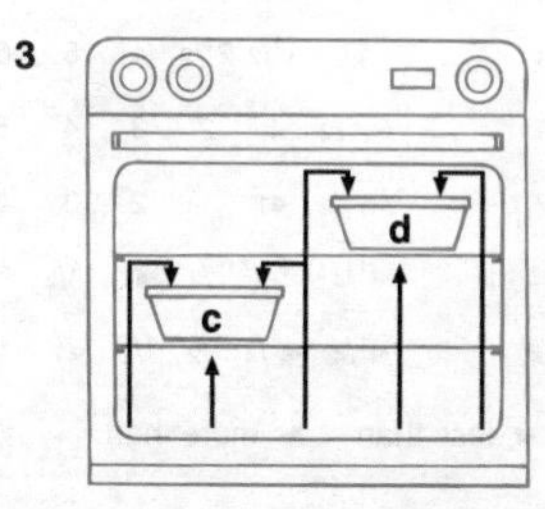
3
d
c

Gas cookers

In standard gas ovens the difference in temperature between the top and bottom shelf positions is much greater than in electric ovens. Most recipes assume that food will be cooked in the centre of the oven. Some recipes specify which shelf should be used.

Shelf temperatures in a gas oven The difference between the oven temperature setting and the actual temperature on each shelf is shown in the diagram below. The actual temperature at the top of a pre-heated oven is higher than the oven temperature setting; the actual temperature at the bottom of the oven is lower than the oven temperature setting.

Shelf temperatures in a gas oven

	Setting									
	¼-½	1	2	3	4	5	6	7	8	9
Top shelf	1½	2	3	4½	5½	6½	8	9	9►	9►
Shelf 2	1	1½	2½	4	5	6	7	8	9	9►
Shelf 3	¼-½	1	2	3	4	5	6	7	8	9
Shelf 4	¼-½	◄1	1	2	3	4	5	5½	6	7
Shelf 5	◄¼	½	½	◄1	1½	2	2½	3½	4½	5
Oven floor	◄¼	◄¼	½	½	◄1	1	1½	2½	3	4

◄ less than ► more than

Microwave cookers

In microwave ovens, microwaves (a form of radiation similar to radio waves) are used to vibrate water molecules in food. The friction created produces heat, which spreads quickly through the food. Microwave cooking is up to 75% faster than conventional methods. However, foods do not turn brown and crispy on the surface. A combination oven combines convected heat (as in ordinary electric ovens) and microwave energy. It has the advantages of both cooking methods.

Microwave oven labels A label is diplayed on most new microwaves. It shows the power output (in watts) of the microwave and the heating category letter (from A–E). This letter can be cross-referenced with the heating instructions given on some ready-meal packs. A Category D oven will heat food faster than a category C oven but not as fast as a category E oven.

An oven label

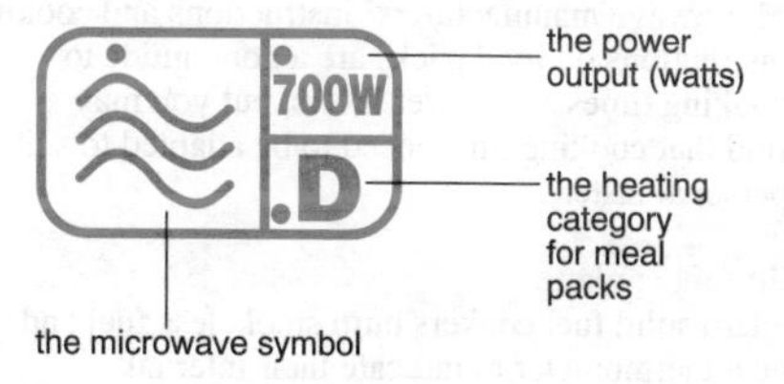

Microwave oven timings The time taken for food to cook inside a microwave oven depends on:

- the nature of the food – foods with a high proportion of water cook faster than dry foods;
- the quantity of food being cooked – 2 lb of potatoes will take more time to cook than 1 lb of potatoes;
- the power of the oven – a 700 W oven is more powerful than a 600 W oven and will cook food more quickly; and
- the power setting used – refer to your microwave instruction manual and follow the manufacturer's advice.

Tips for microwave cooking

- Stir or rearrange food part way through reheating, cooking or defrosting, to make sure the heat is distributed evenly.
- Allow food to stand for a minute or so after cooking – microwaves continue to cook food after the cooking time has ended.
- Microwave manufacturers' instructions and cooking instructions on food packs are a good guide to cooking times and power levels, but you may find that cooking times need to be adapted to suit personal taste.

Solid fuel cookers

Modern solid fuel cookers burn smokeless fuel and have a thermometer to indicate their internal temperature. Many traditional solid fuel ovens have now been converted to run on oil or gas – fuels which give a more adjustable heat output.

Cooking with a solid fuel cooker

- The surface hotplate is usually the same temperature as the oven; neither can be regulated quickly.
- Temperature gradually falls unless new fuel is added.
- Cooking should be planned so that dishes that require a high temperature are cooked first, followed by those requiring a moderate to low heat.
- Note that with each addition of new fuel the temperature falls temporarily.

A solid fuel cooker

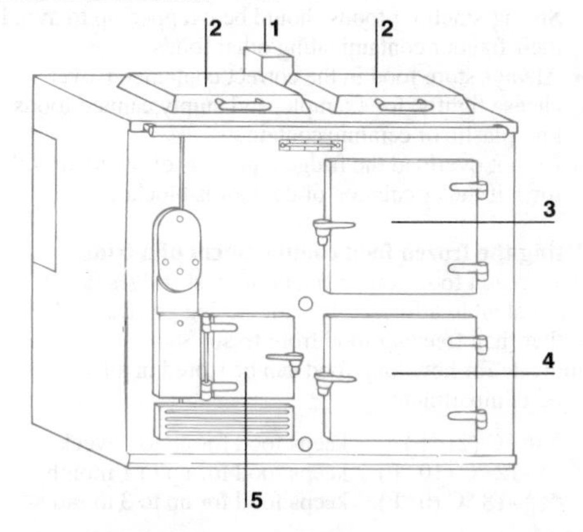

1 Chimney flue outlet
2 Lids over hotplates
3 First oven
4 Second oven
5 Fire door

REFRIGERATORS

A refrigerator's main compartment keeps food at between 0 and 6 °C (32 and 43 °F). At this temperature, the activity of food-spoiling microbes (and therefore food decay) is slowed down but not stopped.

Tips for using a refrigerator

- Never put hot food immediately into the fridge – let it cool first.
- Raw or uncooked foods should be wrapped up so that they cannot touch and contaminate other foods.
- Strong-smelling foods should be wrapped up to avoid their flavour contaminating other foods.
- Always store food in the correct container. Cover cheese tightly, for example, and empty canned foods into plastic or ceramic containers.
- Do not overload the fridge – pockets of warm air will form if the circulation of cool air is blocked.

Using the frozen food compartment of a fridge

The frozen food compartment of most fridges is not equivalent to a freezer. It is for storing pre-frozen food rather than freezing food from fresh. Star ratings indicate for how long food can be stored in a frozen food compartment:

* -6 °C (21 °F)	keeps food for up to 1 week
** -12 °C (10 °F)	keeps food for up to 1 month
*** -18 °C (0 °F)	keeps food for up to 3 months

A freezer compartment with the symbol ****
-23 °C (-9 °F) can be used to freeze food from fresh.

Where to put food in a larder style refrigerator

Larder style refrigerator

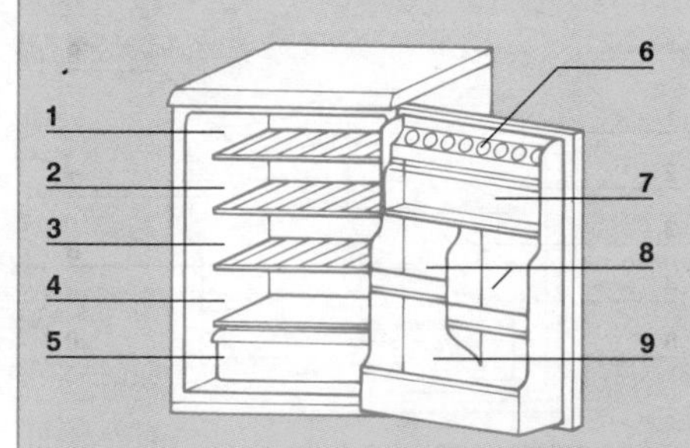

The coldest part of the refrigerator is likely to be the bottom two shelves.

1 Top shelf	Dairy products, jellies, cold desserts
2 Second shelf	Cooked meat, cooked food, leftovers
3 Third shelf	Raw meat, raw fish
4 Fourth shelf	Bottles (laid down)
5 Crisper	Salad, fruit, vegetables
6 Egg rack	Eggs
7 Dairy compartment	Butter, lard, margarine, cheese
8 Commodity rack	Cream, bottled fruit and vegetables, juices
9 Bottle rack	Milk, bottled drinks, cans of beer

Where to put food in a refrigerator with a frozen food compartment

Refrigerator with frozen food compartment

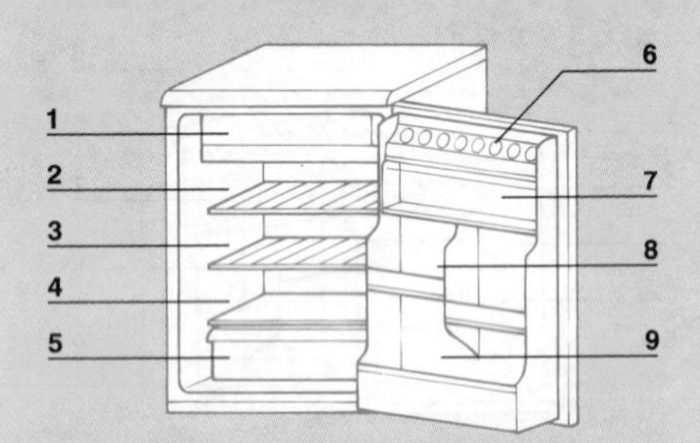

The coldest part of the refrigerator is the frozen food compartment and usually the shelf just below it.

1 Frozen food compartment	Ice cubes, ice-cream, pre-packed frozen food
2 Top shelf	Raw meat, raw fish
3 Second shelf	Cooked meat, cooked food, leftovers
4 Third shelf	Dairy products, jellies, cold desserts
5 Crisper	Salad, fruit, vegetables
6 Egg rack	Eggs
7 Dairy compartment	Butter, lard, margarine, cheese
8 Commodity rack	Cream, bottled fruit and vegetables, juices
9 Bottle rack	Milk, bottled drinks, cans of beer

Food storage times in the main compartment of a fridge

Food	Storage time
Butter	6–8 weeks
Cakes	2 days
Canned ham	6 months
Cheese – hard	1–2 weeks
Cheese – soft	2–3 days
Cold meats (cooked)	2 days
Cooking fat	12 months
Cream	2–3 days
Eggs	4–5 weeks
Fish (uncooked)	1–2 days
Green salads	5–7 days
Green vegetables	5–7 days
Margarine	3–4 weeks
Milk (pasteurized)	2–3 days
Pickles	1 month
Pies	2 days
Poultry (uncooked)	1–2 days
Red meat (uncooked)	2–3 days
Salad dressings	3 months
Shellfish (uncooked)	1 day
Yoghurt	2–3 days
Wine, cooking	1 month
Wine, table	3 days

Note: For more information about storing specific foods, see **Section 4, Food**.

FREEZERS

A freezer keeps food at -18 °C (0 °F). Freezing at this temperature drastically slows the growth of microorganisms and stops the breakdown of nutrients by natural chemicals (enzymes) in food.

Fresh food is best frozen at temperatures between -21 °C (-6 °F) and -23 °C (-9 °F). A freezer with the symbol **** can be used to freeze fresh food.

Tips for home freezing

- Do not put warm foods in the freezer – it creates condensation.
- Keep the freezer filled with food. This helps to lower running costs because food is a better insulator than air.
- Freeze only fresh food that is in good condition.
- Freeze food in small, individual portions to prevent wasting large items when the food defrosts.
- Wrap food in polythene freezer bags or use plastic and polythene containers with snap-on lids.
- Wrap solid foods tightly and exclude air to prevent 'freezer burn' (white spots on the food surface caused by evaporation of water from the food).
- When freezing liquids leave space at the top of the container to allow for expansion.
- Separate items such as hamburgers with a layer of waxed paper to prevent them sticking together.
- Label packages with a description of the contents and the date frozen.

Storing food in a freezer at -18 °C (0 °F)

Food	Maximum storage time	Special thawing instructions
Cakes and pastry	1 month	Thaw in wrapping
Fresh bread	1 month	Thaw in wrapping
Casseroles	1 month	Cook from frozen
Sauces, soups and stock	4 months	Heat gently from frozen
Fish (raw)	6 months	Thaw in wrapping
Shellfish (prefrozen)	3 months	Thaw in wrapping
Bacon	6 months	Thaw in wrapping in refrigerator, allowing 5 hrs per lb (450 g)
Beef	12 months	
Ham (unsliced)	3 months	
Lamb	9 months	
Pork	9 months	
Poultry (4–5 lb)	12 months	Thaw overnight in refrigerator
Turkey (9–10 lb)	12 months	Thaw for 36 hrs in refrigerator

Note: For more information about freezing and thawing specific foods, see **Section 4, Food**.

Power failures

Ideally the contents of your freezer should be insured. In the event of a power failure follow these suggestions to minimize any loss of food. Freezers are well insulated and can maintain a low temperature for several hours as long as they remain sealed.

- Keep the freezer door closed; do not allow warm air into the freezer.
- Food that is thawed at the edge but icy in the centre can be refrozen if it is still cold.
- Fully thawed bread, raw pastry, fruit and cakes can be refrozen.
- Raw meat and fish can be cooked and then refrozen.
- Do not refreeze any other foods.

> *Tip:* Keep a bag of ice cubes on top of your food in the freezer. If the power fails or the door is left ajar the amount the ice cubes have thawed will give you an indication of how severe the problem is.

FOOD PROCESSING MACHINES

Food Processor (**1**) Regarded by many as an essential item in the kitchen. The food processor should have a good bowl capacity (about 1 litre) and a strong motor. The range of functions includes mixing, shredding, slicing, milling, chopping, whisking, blending and chipping.

Mixer Used for mixing, beating and whisking ingredients. A self-standing mixer (**2**) is best for large quantities, but it is probably not worth buying one if you already have a food processor. Hand-held electric whisks (**3**) are useful for smaller volumes and better than food processors for whisking egg whites.

Blender (**4**) Used mainly for puréeing ingredients for e.g. soup. Some blenders have mill attachments for milling nuts, coffee, etc. Hand-held blenders are available (**5**).

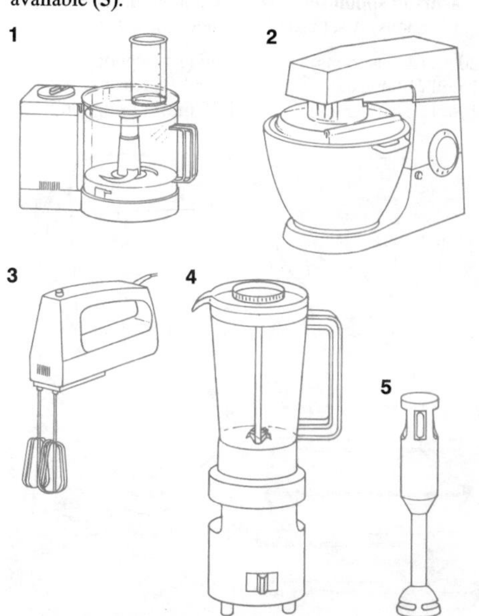

MEASURING AND WEIGHING EQUIPMENT

Measuring jugs (1 & 2) Available in various sizes. Jugs with both imperial and metric graduations are the most useful.

Measuring spoon set (3 & 4) Available in sets of four or six spoons. A set usually includes these sizes:

20 ml (4 teaspoons)
15 ml (1 tablespoon)
10 ml (2 teaspoons)
5 ml (1 teaspoon)
2.5 ml (½ teaspoon)
1.25 ml (¼ teaspoon)

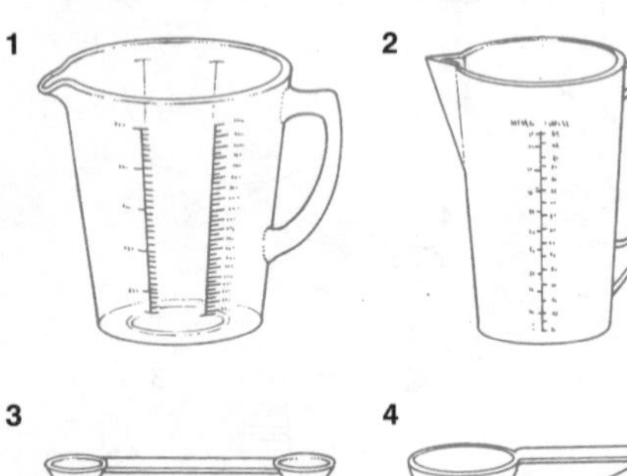

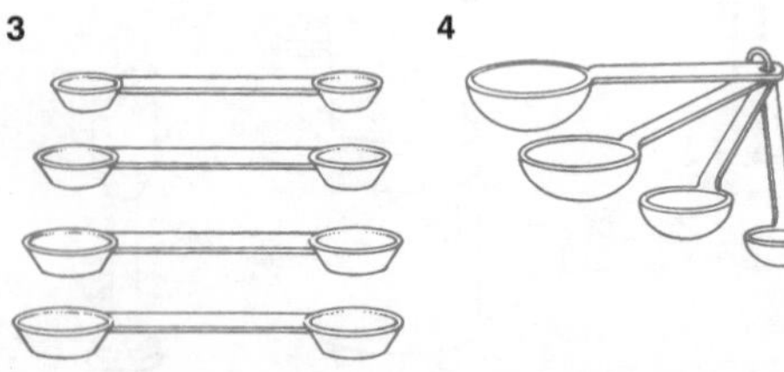

Scales Balance scales (**5**) are the most accurate but are expensive. They can be used with imperial or metric weights. Spring scales (**6**) are more common but less sturdy. Remember to check the setting is at zero each time you use them. Electronic scales (**7**) which give very accurate measurements are also available. Wall-mounted scales are handy and save on work surface space. To be practical, scales should have 25g/1 oz graduations and be able to weigh up to 5 kg (10 lb).

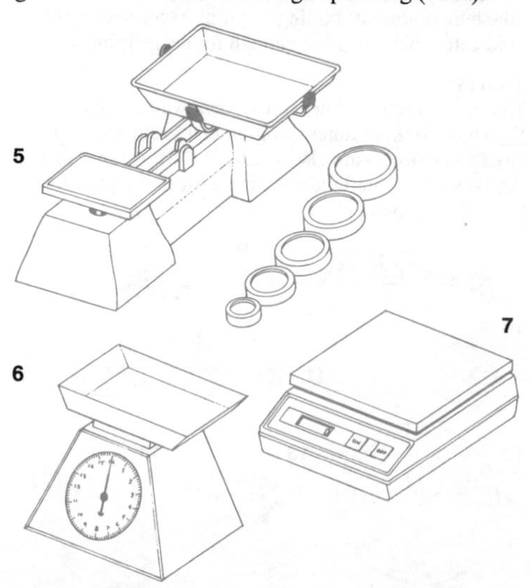

Thermometers:

Oven thermometer (8) Use if accurate measurement of oven temperature is needed – oven thermostats are usually not very accurate.

Freezer thermometer (9) For checking your freezer temperature.

Meat thermometer (10) Insert into roasting meat to check its internal temperature.

Sugar or deep-fat thermometer (11) Use to measure the temperature of boiling sugar in sweet-making or to indicate when fat is hot enough for deep-frying.

Timers

The most practical timer is a kitchen wall clock (**12**). For short cooking times, programmable electronic or clockwork timers are also available (**13**). A timer that can be worn around the neck is useful if you have to leave the kitchen (**14**).

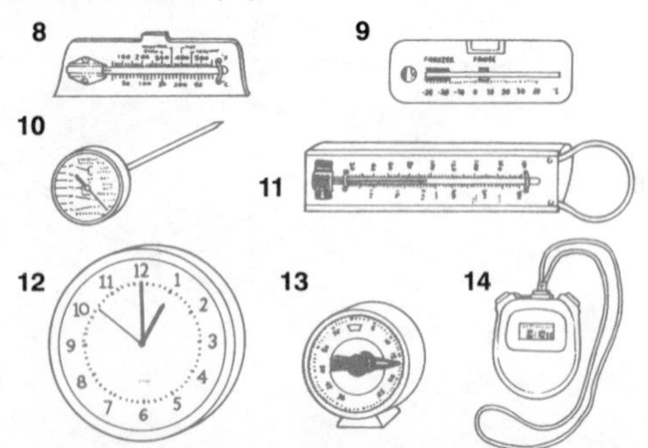

POTS AND PANS

Casserole set (1) Use enamelled iron or ovenproof glazed earthenware for long, slow cooking in the oven.

Double saucepan (2) The inner pan is warmed indirectly by heating water in the outer pan. Use to gently heat delicate sauces, to make egg custard and for melting chocolate without burning.

Egg poacher (3) Eggs are cooked gently in non-stick moulds which are heated by simmering water in the pan below.

Frying pans:

Crêpe pan (4) A small rounded-edge pan for making French pancakes.

Deep-fat frying pan (5) The high sides stop fat

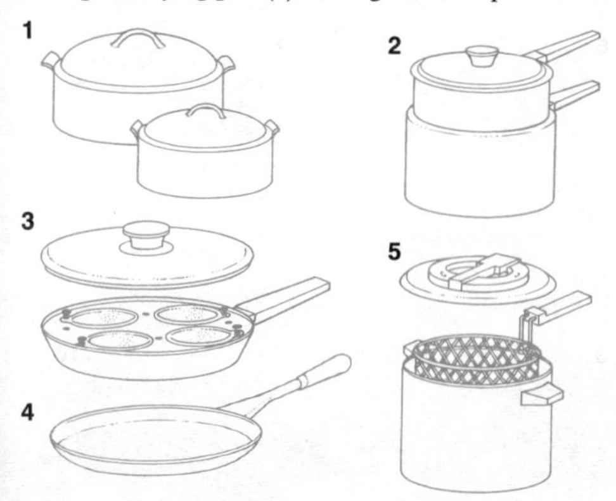

spillage while frying and allow food to be completely immersed in the fat.

Omelette pan (6) The base curves gently into the sides to make folding and serving omelettes easier.

Pizza plate (7) The raised edges help to retain the pizza topping.

Pressure cooker (8) By increasing internal pressure the temperature at which water boils inside the pressure cooker is raised. This allows foods which are usually boiled, stewed or steamed to be cooked much more quickly.

Roasting tin and rack Use a tin **(9)** appropriate to the size of the roast; a small roast in a large pan will dry out and burn because the juices will be allowed to spread too thinly. The rack **(10)** fits inside the tin.

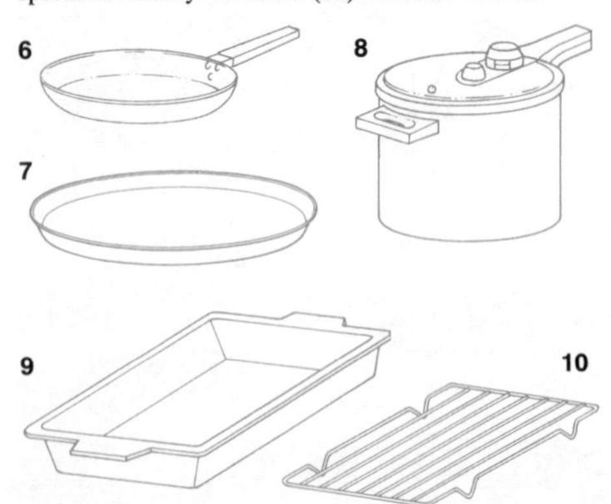

Saucepan set (11) Pans are made of cast iron (plain or enamelled), stainless or enamelled steel, aluminium, copper, porcelain or glass. Buy good quality, durable pans. Unlined aluminium pans can turn some foods a greyish colour. Glass pans do not conduct heat well.
Sauté pan (12) The high sides allow you to toss food while frying over high heat.
Splash guard (13) Use to cover pans to stop splashing while allowing steam to escape.
Steamers:
Chinese rice steamer (14) Attaches to the side of a saucepan and is used for steaming rice.
Folding steaming platform (15) The adjustable folding side panels ensure that the steamer can fit into

any size of saucepan.

Fish kettle (16) Fish is placed on a steaming-platform inside the fish kettle.

Vegetable steamer (17) Several different vegetables can be steamed simultaneously in the perforated pans which fit over the hot water pan. Put vegetables that require the longest cooking time in the lowest pan.

Stock pot (18) Use a stock pot with a heavy lid for long, slow cooking. The deep, straight sides ensure minimum evaporation of liquid.

Wok (19) A heavy stainless-steel wok is best; light aluminium woks do not distribute heat evenly and tend to burn some of their contents while undercooking the rest.

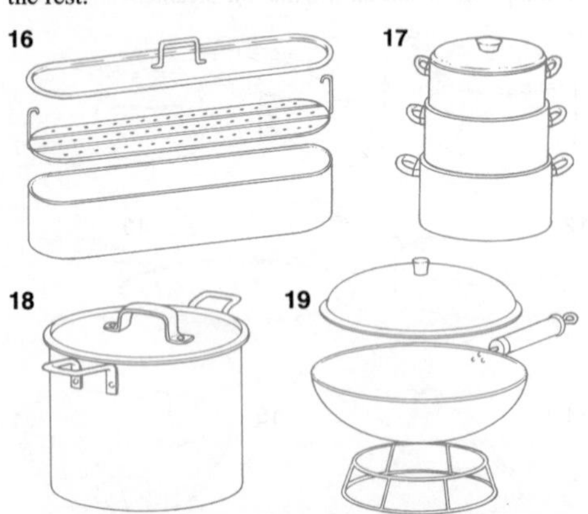

KNIVES AND OTHER CUTTING TOOLS

Apple corer (1) Removes a cylindrical section from the apple centre, leaving the rest of the fruit intact.
Boning knife (2) The rigidity of the blade should match the rigidity of the bones. For boning large cuts of meat, use a strong rigid blade; for delicate fowl, e.g. chickens and pigeons, use a more flexible blade.
Bread knife (3) The serrated edge allows bread to be cut evenly with a sawing action.
Canelling knife (4) The sharpened notch is used to cut decorative grooves in pastry edges, etc.
Carving knife and fork (5 & 6) Always sharpen a carving knife before use; a very sharp knife is less likely to slip. The long prongs of the carving fork hold the meat steady while it is being carved. The guard protects the hand from an accidential slip of the knife.
Cheese knife (7) Used for cutting and serving cheese. The prongs on the end of the blade can be used to skewer a slice of cheese.

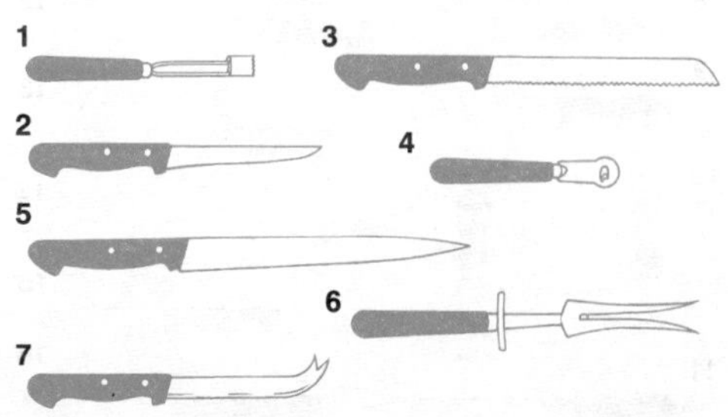

Citrus zester (8) Scrape the zester along the surface of a citrus fruit to remove the zest in thin slithers.
Cleaver/chopper (9) Swing the chopper downwards onto the food, letting its weight do the splitting and cutting. Use on bones or for general chopping.
Double-handled chopper (10) Use a rocking motion to finely chop herbs.
Filleting knife (11) A straight-edged, flexible blade used for filleting fish.
Freezer knife (12) This strong and flexible serrated knife is used to cut through frozen foods or to separate foods which have become frozen together.
Fruit knife (13) The sharp serrated blade can cut fruit without squashing its delicate flesh.
General purpose knives Use large sized blades **(14)** for chopping and smaller blades **(15)** for fine work, e.g. dicing vegetables.
Grapefruit knife (16) Used to prepare a grapefruit for eating by loosening each section of fruit from the rind.

Graters A steel box-shaped grater **(17)** is ideal for general purpose use. For efficient cheese grating use a hand-operated rotary grater **(18)**. A small conical grater is handy for nutmeg **(19)**.
Grinder (20) A manually operated rotary action grinder is useful for grinding meat, cracking nuts and roughly crushing other hard foods.
Ham knife (21) Indentations on the blade reduce friction, helping to keep thin slices intact. This knife can also be used to cut smoked salmon.
Lobster crackers (22) Used to crack lobster claws.
Lobster pick (23) Used to prise out the meat from inside lobster claws.

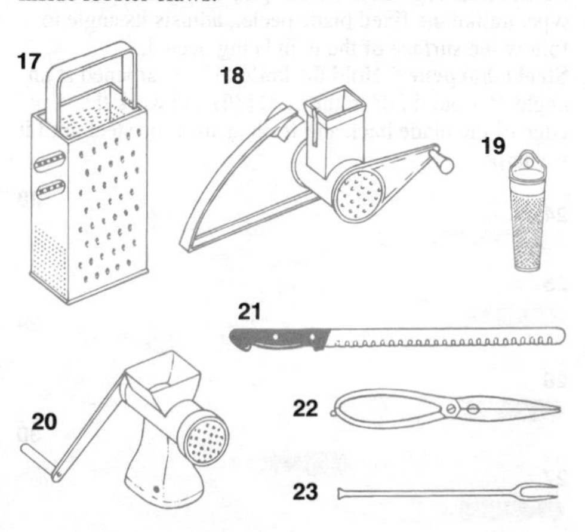

Melon baller (24) The circular metal scoop extracts ball-shaped pieces from melons and potatoes.
Oyster knife (25) A short, rigid blade for levering open oysters.
Palette knife (26) The flexible, blunt-edged blade can be used to fold, mix, spread and scrape soft mixtures, and to lift or flip thin baked foods.
Paring knife (27) Has a short, sharp blade for peeling fruit or vegetables.
Poultry shears (28) Used to cut feathers from poultry or game birds. The notch cracks bones and one of the blades is usually serrated for cutting cartilage.
Potato and vegetable peeler (29) The swivel blade type, unlike the fixed blade peeler, adjusts its angle to follow the surface of the item being peeled.
Steel (sharpener) Hold the knife to be sharpened at an angle of around 20° to the steel **(30)** and work the very edge of the blade back and forth against the steel until it is sharp.

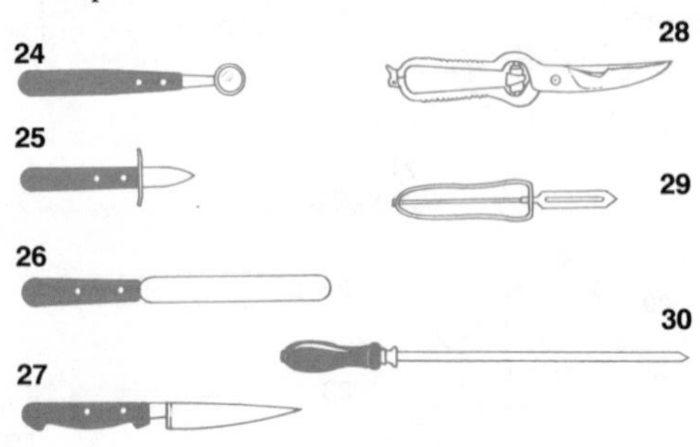

BAKEWARE AND MOULDS

Baking sheet (1) A lipped baking sheet is useful when an overflow is likely. A smooth-edged baking sheet allows the finished product to be slid off easily.

Bun tin (2) A tray with rows of individual cake moulds for making batches of small cakes, batters, buns, pies and tarts.

Cake tin (3) A round tin used for baking cakes.

Cake tin with spring-clip (4) When the clip is unfastened the sides of the tin expand by 12 mm (1/2 in), making the extraction of fragile cakes simpler.

Cooling rack (5) A rectangular or circular grid allows air to circulate all around a cake left to cool.

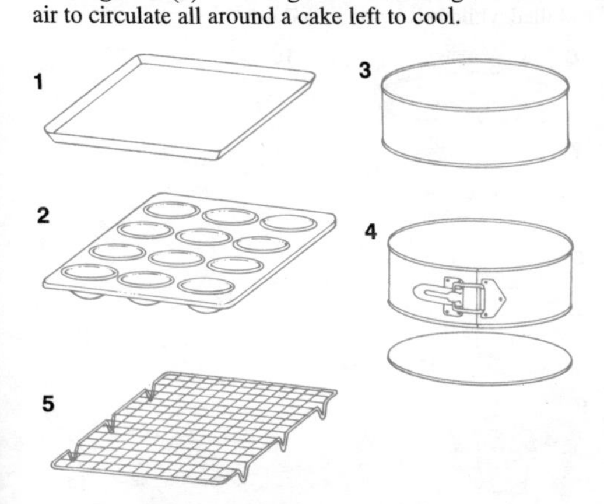

Flan rings Plain (**6**) or fluted (**7**) and available in a wide range of sizes.
Flour dredger or sifter (**8**) Lightly shake the flour from the dredger for a smooth sprinkling.
Jelly moulds (**9**) A variety of decorative moulds are available in plastic, aluminium and tin-lined copper.
Loaf tin (**10**) Used for baking bread. High sides allow room for the loaf to rise.
Mixing bowl A large ceramic bowl (**11**) is best for mixing large quantities because its weight keeps it stable. Smaller glass or plastic bowls (**12**) are handy for everyday use.
Pastry board (**13**) A slab of marble keeps dough chilled while it is being rolled out.

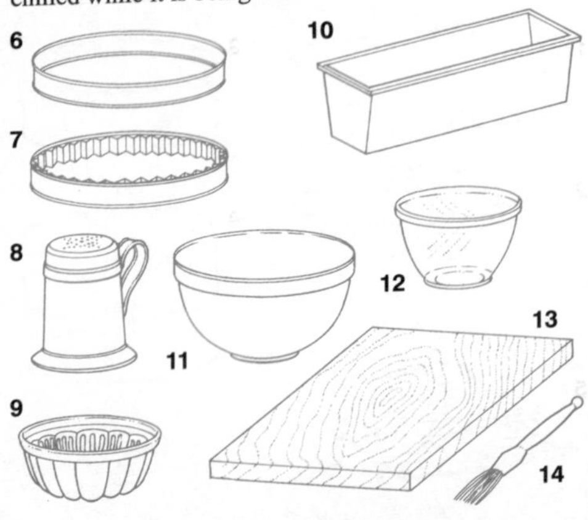

Pastry brush (14) Use different pastry brushes for brushing egg or milk onto pastry, for greasing pans and for brushing marinade onto meats.
Pastry cutters (15) Cutters are available in a huge variety of shapes and sizes.
Pie dish (16) A deep, ceramic dish for all kinds of pies.
Piping bag (17) A nylon bag with interchangeable metal nozzles for piping cake icing, cream, etc.
Raised pie tins (18 & 19) The detachable sides allow baking of traditional pies with high pastry sides.
Ramekin dishes (20) Small, ovenproof soufflé dishes used for preparing and serving individual portions.

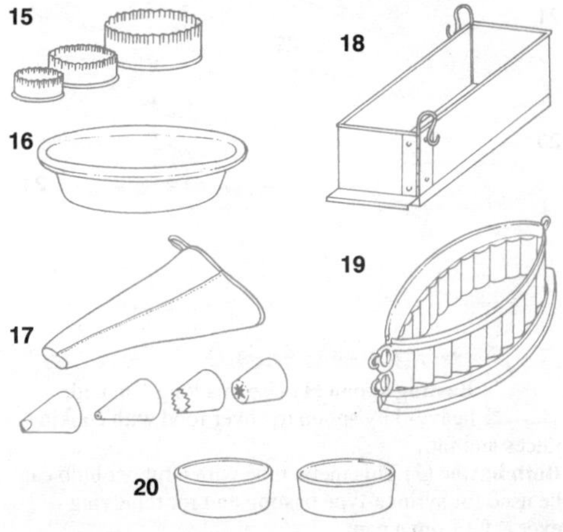

Rolling pin (21) Use a smooth, easy-to-clean wooden, ceramic or glass pin for rolling out pastry. A heavy rolling pin makes the job easier.
Sandwich tins (22) Two are needed to make a Victoria sponge cake.
Soufflé dish (23) A porcelain dish with high sides helps to support a soufflé as it rises.
Tube tin (24) The funnel helps to distribute heat and cook the inside of the cake.

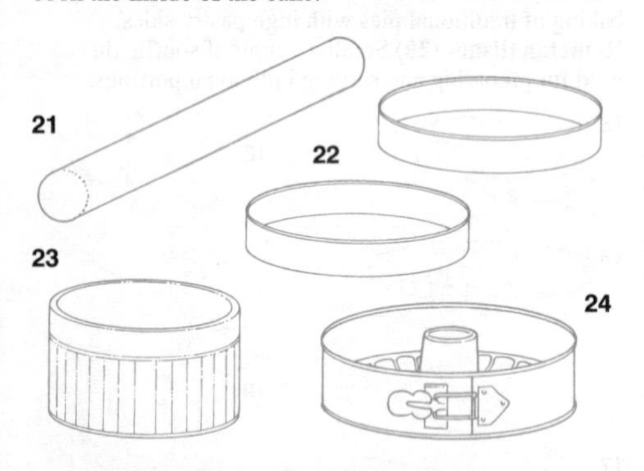

OTHER HAND TOOLS

Basting spoon (1) Use this long-handled, heavy-duty spoon to cover food with cooking juices and fat.
Bulb baster (2) This metal tube with a rubber bulb can be used for syringe-type basting and for removing excess fat from a pan.

Colander (3) An invaluable tool for washing and draining food.

Conical strainer or chinois (4) A metal, reinforced strainer that fits over a bowl and can be used to make purées.

Cutlet bat (5) Made of metal or wood. Use this bat to pound and flatten certain cuts of meat before cooking.

Fish slice (6) Used to gently lift and turn fish.

Funnel (7) Use a funnel to avoid spillage when pouring a liquid from a pan into a bottle.

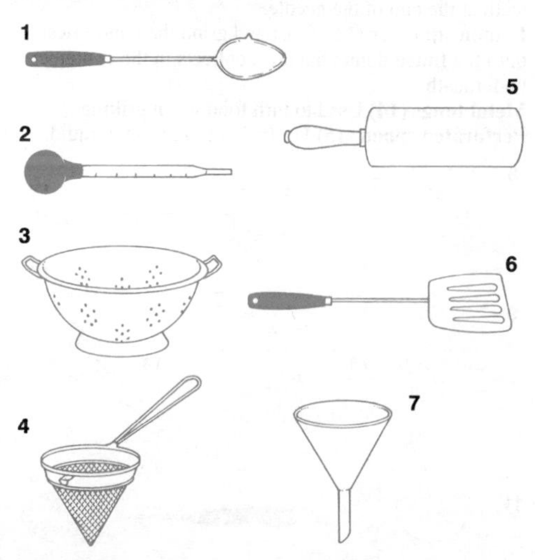

Garlic press (8) Heavy plastic, easy-to-clean models are best.
Ice-cream scoop (9) Used to create ball-shaped servings of ice-cream.
Jam skimmer (10) A flat, perforated spoon used to remove scum from liquid jams and stock.
Ladle (11) Its long handle and large bowl makes this an ideal implement for serving soups and stews.
Larding needle (12) Use to thread streaky bacon through meat – the lengths of bacon are gripped by teeth at the end of the needle.
Lemon squeezer (13) Twist and grind the lemon flesh onto the fluted dome; the juice collects in the container underneath.
Metal tongs (14) Used to turn food when grilling.
Perforated spoon (15) For lifting food from a liquid.

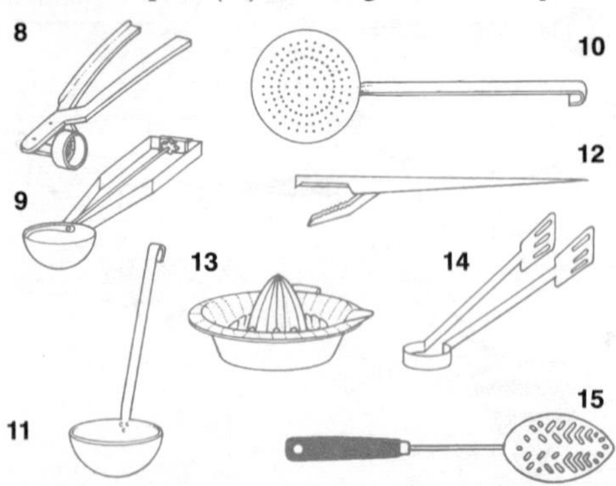

Pestle and mortar Grind spices and nuts yourself to ensure fresher results. Use the pestle **(16)** to grind food in the stone mortar **(17)**.
Pastry scraper (18) A square piece of metal with a wooden handle for scraping scraps of dough or pastry off pastry boards.
Potato masher (19) Used for puréeing potatoes.
Salad spinner (20) Dry salad by spinning it in this hand-operated centrifuge. Water is flung out of the washed salad as the inner plastic basket rotates.
Sieve (21) A stainless steel or nylon bowl-shaped sieve for sifting lumps from flour, etc. Double-mesh sieves are used for fine puréeing.
Skewers (22) Used to hold meat in shape or to skewer kebabs for grilling.
Spaghetti rake (23) A large, wooden, pronged implement for lifting spaghetti.
Spatulas A rubber spatula **(24)** is useful for scraping

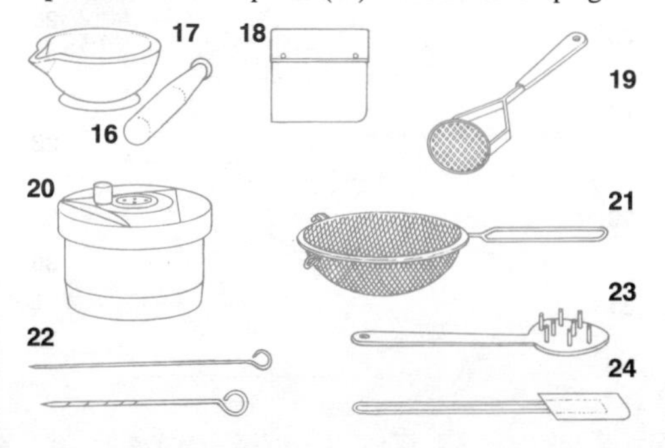

food from bowls or smoothing icing; a wooden spatula (**25**) can be used to remove food from frying pans without scratching their non-stick surfaces.
Tenderizing mallet (**26**) Used for flattening and tenderizing meat by breaking down meat fibres.
Trussing needle (**27**) Used to sew up stuffed meat and poultry.
Whisks:
Balloon whisk (**28**) A heavy whisk for beating air into egg whites, batter, etc.
Flat whisk (**29**) For shallow whisking, e.g. to mix liquid ingredients in the bottom of a pan.
Sauce whisk (**30**) A small whisk for removing lumps from sauces.
Wooden spoons (**31** & **32**) Ideal for stirring and mixing because they do not scratch pans. Wood is liable to absorb the flavours or odours of foods so keep several wooden spoons for different ingredients.

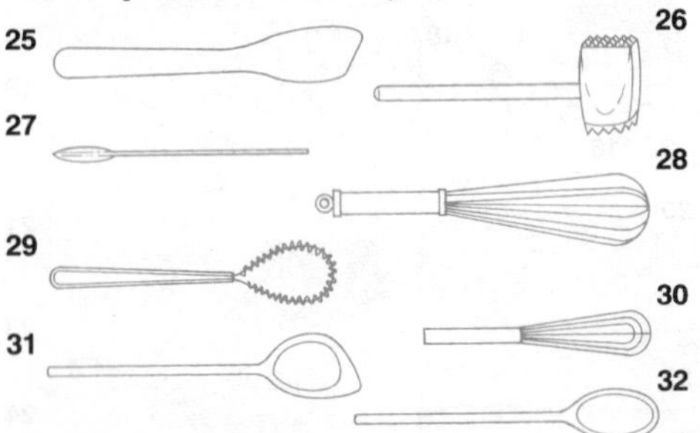

4. Food and drink

This section covers each of the major food groups in detail. It is divided into ten subsections headed *Meat*, *Poultry and game*, *Seafood*, *Vegetables and fruit*, *Nuts and pulses*, *Herbs and spices*, *Dairy products*, *Miscellaneous foods*, *Alcoholic drink* and *Tea and coffee*. Each subsection includes details of food types, buying tips, storage techniques and cooking times. Information is presented in concise bulleted points or easy-to-read tables, and relevant topics are treated consistently for each food group.

MEAT
See p. 82

POULTRY AND GAME
See p. 93

SEAFOOD
See p. 105

VEGETABLES AND FRUIT
See p. 115

NUTS AND PULSES
See p. 140

HERBS AND SPICES
See p. 144

DAIRY PRODUCTS
See p. 151

MISCELLANEOUS FOODS
See p. 159

ALCOHOLIC DRINK
See p. 175

TEA AND COFFEE
See p. 188

MEAT
Cuts of meat and cooking methods

Pork cuts and cooking methods

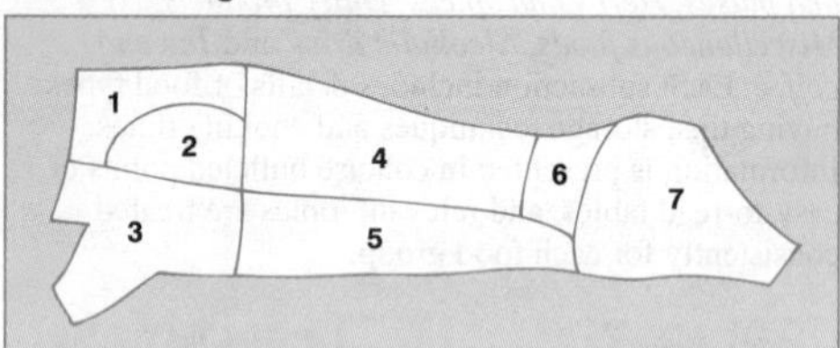

Type of cut	Cooking method
1 Spare rib	Roast, fry, grill, braise
2 Blade bone	Roast, braise, pot-roast, stew
3 Hand and spring	Roast, stew
4 Loin (and kidney)	Roast, fry, grill
5 Belly	Roast, fry, grill, braise, stew
6 Chump end	Roast, fry, grill
7 Leg	Roast

Bacon, gammon and ham cuts and cooking methods

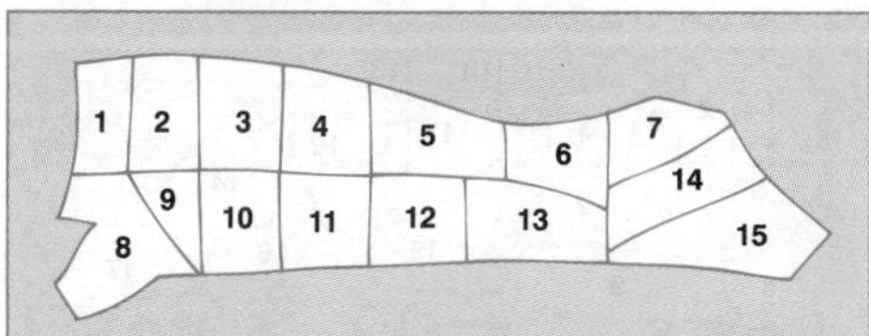

Type of cut	Cooking method
1 End collar	Boil
2 Prime collar	Boil, roast
3 Thick back	Grill
4 Back and ribs	Boil, braise, bake
5 Prime loin	Bake, grill
6 Long back	Fry, grill
7 Corner gammon	Boil, bake
8 Fore hock	Stew
9 Fore slipper	Boil
10 Thick streaky	Fry, grill
11 Prime streaky	Fry, grill
12 Thin streaky	Fry, grill (mainly fatty)
13 Flank	Fry, grill
14 Middle gammon	Boil, bake, grill, fry
15 Gammon hock	Boil

Beef cuts and cooking methods

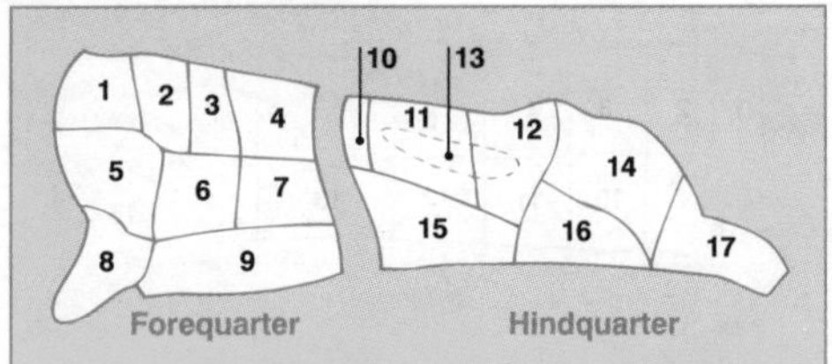

Forequarter

Type of cut	Cooking method
1 Neck	Stew
2 Chuck and blade	Braise, pot-roast, stew
3 Back ribs	Braise, pot-roast
4 Fore ribs	Roast
5 Clod	Stew
6 Top and thick ribs	Braise, pot-roast
7 Thin ribs	Braise, pot-roast
8 Shin	Stew
9 Brisket	Braise, pot-roast, boil

Hindquarter

Type of cut	Cooking method
10 Wing ribs	Roast, grill
11 Sirloin	Roast, grill
12 Rump	Fry, grill
13 Fillet	Grill

continued

Beef cuts and cooking methods (continued)

Type of cut	Cooking method
14 Topside/ Silverside	Roast, pot-roast/ Roast, boil
15 Thin flank	Braise, boil
16 Top rump	Fry, grill, braise
17 Leg	Casserole, stew

Lamb cuts and cooking methods

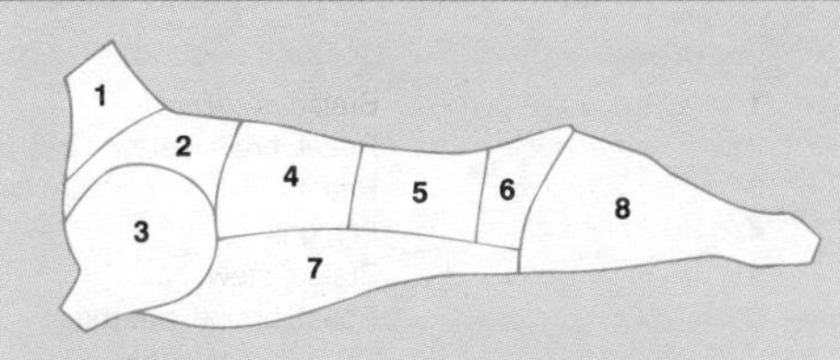

Type of cut	Cooking method
1 Scrag end of neck	Stew
2 Middle neck	Stew
3 Shoulder	Roast, braise, pot-roast
4 Best end neck	Roast, fry, grill
5 Loin } saddle	Roast, fry, grill
6 Chump } saddle	Roast, fry, grill
7 Breast	Roast, braise, stew, pot-roast
8 Leg	Roast, braise, boil, pot-roast

Veal cuts and cooking methods

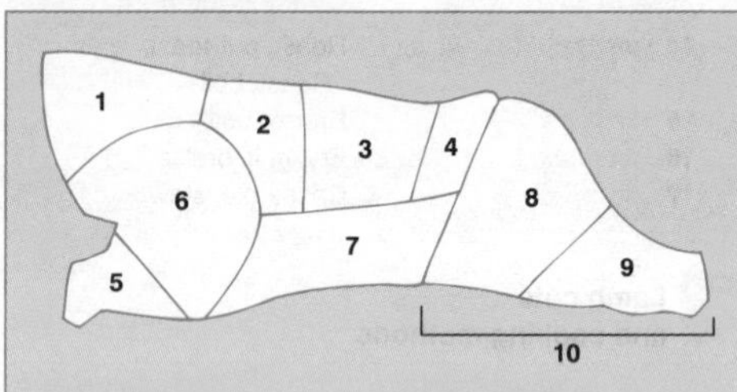

Type of cut	Cooking method
1 Scrag end of neck	Braise, stew
2 Best end of neck	Roast, braise, stew
3 Loin	Roast
4 Chump chops	Fry, grill
5 Knuckle	Braise, stew, boil
6 Shoulder without knuckle	Roast, braise, pot-roast
7 Breast	Roast, braise
8 Fillet	Roast
9 Knuckle	Braise, pot-roast, stew, boil
10 Leg of veal (8 & 9)	Roast

Buying meat

Tips for buying fresh meat

- Buy fresh meat the day before you intend to use it; the longer meat is stored in a refrigerator the less satisfactory the cooking results.
- Make sure you choose a cut of meat suitable to the cooking method and dish you have in mind.
- Boned meat is easier to carve than meat still on the bone. Bones can be used to make stocks and soups so you may want to ask your butcher for any that have been removed.
- Meat should be firm, moist and free from odour. There should be no dry patches or discoloration.
- Good meat should contain some fat; this makes it more tender and tasty when cooked than very lean meat.
- Fat should be firm and not oily.

Meat tenderness Meat is muscle. Some muscles are worked harder than others and are, therefore, tougher. Muscle on older animals has been worked for longer and is tougher than on young animals. The price of various cuts of meat reflect this, with the tenderest parts of young animals being the most expensive. Older meat and cheaper cuts can be very good value if used in slow cooking recipes.

Storing meat

Tips for keeping fresh meat before cooking

- Remove any plastic wrapping immediately.
- Handle as little as possible to reduce risk of transferring bacteria to or from the meat.

- Cover meat with cooking foil or greased paper to prevent it drying out in the fridge.
- Store meat in the coldest part of the fridge.

Meat storage times

In the fridge	Duration
Cold meats (cooked)	2 days
Mince (uncooked)	1 day
Red meats (uncooked)	2–3 days
Sausages (uncooked)	1–2 days
In the freezer	**Duration**
Bacon rashers	6 months
Bacon joint	3 months
Beef	8–12 months
Lamb	6–9 months
Mince	2–3 months
Pork	6–9 months
Sausages	2–3 months
Veal	6–9 months

Tips for thawing meat

- Frozen joints of meat cook more evenly if thoroughly defrosted. Thaw in the fridge, then allow to reach room temperature just before cooking.
- Many microwave ovens have a defrost option which greatly reduces the defrosting time needed for meat joints. Always follow the manufacturer's instructions carefully.
- Chops, steaks and sausages can be cooked directly from the freezer but will take longer to cook than thawed meat.

Thawing times for meat

In the fridge	Duration
Joints	
• less than 1.5 kg (3 lbs)	3–4 hours per 500 g (1 lb)
• more than 1.5 kg (3 lbs)	4–7 hours per 500 g (1 lb)
Steaks and chops	6–8 hours
Stewing/braising cuts and mince	8–12 hours
Sausages	4–6 hours

Cooking meat

Tips for roasting meat

The heat needed to roast a joint of meat means that it is likely to dry out. To avoid this:

- Only roast the tenderest cuts of meat, which have been specifically prepared as joints.
- Put animal or vegetable fat on the joint.
- Wrap the joint in cooking foil, put it in a roasting bag or use a roasting pan with a transparent lid so that juices cannot escape. Foil should be removed from a joint 20–30 minutes before the end of the cooking time to allow the meat to brown on the surface.
- Baste the joint regularly with the juices that collect in its cooking tray and extra melted fat if necessary.

Roasting times for meat

Meat	Fast roast 220 °C (425 °F) gas mark 7	Slow roast 190 °C (375 °F) gas mark 5
Pork		
• on the bone	25 mins/454 g (1 lb) + 25 mins	
• off the bone		35 mins/454 g (1 lb) + 35 mins

continued

Roasting times for meat (continued)

Meat	Fast roast 220 °C (425 °F) gas mark 7	Slow roast 180 °C (350 °F) gas mark 4
Beef		
• on the bone	15 mins/454 g (1 lb) + 15 mins	20 mins/454 g (1 lb) + 20 mins
• off the bone	20 mins/454 g (1 lb) + 20 mins	30 mins/454 g (1 lb) + 30 mins
Lamb		
• on the bone	20 mins/454 g (1 lb) + 20 mins	25 mins/454 g (1 lb) + 25 mins
• off the bone	25 mins/454 g (1 lb) + 25 mins	35 mins/454 g (1 lb) + 35 min
Veal		
• on the bone	25 mins/454 g (1 lb) + 25 mins	35 mins/454 g (1 lb) + 35 mins
• off the bone	30 mins/454 g (1 lb) + 30 mins	40 mins/454 g (1 lb) + 40 mins

Note: **Fast roasting** Uses a high temperature over a short period. This seals the surface of the meat quickly and helps to preserve flavour. However, it causes the joint to shrink and should only be used with the tenderest meat.
Slow roasting Uses a low temperature over a long period. This reduces shrinkage of the joint and helps to tenderize the meat.

Grilling and frying times for meat

Meat	Duration
Pork	
• Chops	15–20 mins
• Sausages	10–15 mins
Bacon	
• Rashers	5–10 mins
• Chops	10–15 mins
Gammon	
• Steaks	10–15 mins
Beef	
• Steaks	Rare: 7 mins Medium: 10 mins Well done: 15 mins
Lamb	
• Cutlets	7–10 mins
• Chops	12–15 mins
• Kidneys	5–10 mins
• Liver	4–6 mins
Veal	
• Chops	12–15 mins
• Escalopes	2 mins each side

Boiling times for meat

Meat	Duration
Pork	20 mins/454 g (1 lb) + 20 mins
Cured bacon and ham	25 mins/454 g (1 lb) + 25 mins
Beef	20 mins/454 g (1 lb) + 20 mins
Salt beef	25 mins/454 g (1 lb) + 25 mins
Mutton	20 mins/454 g (1 lb) + 20 mins
Veal	20 mins/454 g (1 lb) + 20 mins

POULTRY AND GAME

Types of poultry and game

Poultry

Includes any domesticated bird bred to provide food. Common poultry include chicken, turkey, duck and goose.

According to recent EU regulations, poultry must be sold with its innards (giblets) removed.

Ready to cook poultry has been plucked and has had its head, feet and innards removed. It is sold whole, disjointed, halved or quartered. It may be sold fresh or frozen.

Chicken sizes

Chickens are categorized according to size:

Poussin Four to six weeks old and weighing no more than 454 g (1 lb). Suitable for roasting, spitting or grilling.

Spring chicken About six weeks old and weighing about 1.25 kg (2½ lb). Best roasted.

Roasting chicken About 8 weeks old and weighing 1.5–2 kg (3–4 lb). Usually roasted whole or fried, grilled or baked in joints.

Boiling fowl Older birds (usually hens after one laying season), about 8 months old. Average weight 2.7 kg (6 lb). Used for stews and casseroles.

Capon A young (10–12 week old) male bird bred to provide a high proportion of meat. Usually 3–4 kg (6–8 lb). Excellent for roasting.

Game
Includes any wild animal hunted for food. Usually divided into feathered game (birds) and furred game (other animals). Common feathered game include grouse, mallard, partridge, pheasant, pigeon and quail. Common furred game include hare, rabbit and deer.

Buying poultry and game

Tips for buying fresh chickens

- Breast and legs should be plump.
- Meat should be firm and white.
- The feet, beak and breastbone should be pliable.
- There should be no bruising or discoloration of the wings.
- The skin and crop should be clean and there should be no feathers remaining.

Tips for buying feathered game Young game birds have the tastiest and tenderest flesh. The *bursa* test can be used to check their age. Game birds have a passage called the bursa between their anus and tail, which shortens with age. Using a matchstick, check the depth of the bursa. On young birds it should be as follows:

- Grouse 1 cm (½ in)
- Partridge 1 cm (½ in)
- Pheasant 2.5 cm (1 in)

Gaming seasons In Britain, most game animals can only be hunted during strictly defined gaming seasons. Purchasers should be aware that game animals offered for sale outside their permitted gaming season may have been frozen for long periods or obtained illegally.

Gaming seasons

Feathered game		Season
Grouse		12 Aug–10 Dec
Mallard		1 Sep–28 Feb
Partridge		1 Sep–31 Jan
Pheasant		1 Oct–31 Jan
Pigeon		No closed season
Furred game		**Season**
Hare		No closed season
Rabbit		No closed season
Deer (venison)		
• Red	male	21 Oct–31 Jul
	female	16 Feb–31 Oct
• Fallow	male	1 May–31 Jul
	female	16 Feb–31 Oct
• Roe	male	21 Oct–31 Mar
	female	1 Mar–31 Oct

Hanging game To get the best flavour from game it must be hung. This allows time for natural enzymes to work on the flesh of the dead animal. Most suppliers provide game that has already been hung. If you want to hang your own game you will need a cool, well ventilated space with no flies. If you do decide to try hanging game, check with your supplier how long the game you buy has already hung.

Hanging times for game

Feathered game	Duration
Grouse	3–8 days
Mallard	1 day
Partridge	3–4 days
Pheasant	7 days
Pigeon	1 day
Quail	No hanging
Furred game	**Duration**
Hare	5–10 days
Rabbit	No hanging
Deer (venison)	7+ days

Note: This table is primarily a guide to help you ensure that any game you buy has been properly hung. Hanging game properly is a considerable skill; air temperature, humidity and other factors can all affect the length of time that game should be hung.

Storing poultry and game

Storage times for poultry and feathered game

In the fridge	Duration
Uncooked poultry and feathered game	1–2 days
In the freezer	**Duration**
Chicken	9–12 months
Turkey	9–12 months
Goose	4–6 months
Duck/Mallard	3 months
Other feathered game	4–6 months

Storage times for furred game

In the freezer	Duration
Hare	6–8 months
Rabbit	4–6 months
Venison	6–8 months

Note: See also **Hanging game** (pp. 96–7).

Tips for thawing poultry and game

- Frozen poultry and game birds must be thawed thoroughly before cooking, otherwise those parts which are not completely thawed will not be heated sufficiently during cooking to ensure that harmful organisms are destroyed.
- Thawing at room temperature is quicker but less safe than thawing in a fridge. At room temperature there is a risk that parts of the bird will become warm enough to encourage the growth of dangerous organisms before the whole bird is thawed.
- Many microwaves have a defrost setting which greatly reduces thawing time. Always follow the instructions given in your microwave handbook.

Thawing times for poultry

Weight	In the fridge	Room temperature
900 g (2 lb)	28 hours	8 hours
1.35 kg (3 lb)	32 hours	9 hours
1.80 kg (4 lb)	38 hours	10 hours
2.25 kg (5 lb)	44 hours	12 hours
2.70 kg (6 lb)	50 hours	14 hours
3.15 kg (7 lb)	56 hours	16 hours
4.23 kg (9 lb)	65 hours	19 hours
5.40 kg (12 lb)	70 hours	22 hours
6.75 kg (15 lb)	75 hours	24 hours
8.10 kg (18 lb)	80 hours	27 hours
9.90 kg (22 lb)	96 hours	36 hours

Thawing times for game

In the fridge	Duration
Game birds	*See* **Thawing times for poultry** table (p. 99)
Rabbit/hare	4–6 hours
Venison	6–8 hours

Cooking poultry and game

Tips for roasting poultry and feathered game

- Chicken and turkey can easily become dry when roasted. To prevent this, wrap the bird in foil, or use a roasting bag or lidded pan to retain moisture (foil should be removed 20 minutes before the end of the cooking time to allow browning). Alternatively, baste the bird every 15 minutes with the juices in the roasting tin and additional melted fat if necessary.
- If the bird is to be stuffed take into account the extra weight of the stuffing when calculating the cooking time.
- Duck is a very fatty bird and does not need basting or wrapping during roasting. The skin should be pricked to allow fat to run out during cooking and the bird should be on a rack so that it is raised out of the liquid fat that collects in the roasting tray.
- Goose and game birds should be barded with strips of bacon or pork fat and basted frequently to keep them moist. Remove barding strips before the end of the cooking time to allow the skin to brown.

Tips for roasting furred game

- Only roast young and tender hares or rabbits. Older animals are most suitable for casseroles.
- Hares and rabbits should be barded with strips of bacon or pork fat and basted frequently to keep them moist.
- Venison joints should be coated with a paste of flour and water to keep them moist. Scrape the paste off 20 minutes before the end of the cooking time to allow the meat to brown.

Poultry roasting times

Type	Oven setting	Duration
Chicken	190 °C (375 °F) gas mark 5	20 mins/454g (1 lb) + 20 mins
Duck	200 °C (400 °F) gas mark 6	20 mins/454 g (1 lb)
Goose	Fast roast 200 °C (400 °F) gas mark 6	15 mins/454 g (1 lb) + 15 mins
	Slow roast 180 °C (350 °F) gas mark 4	25 mins/454 g (1 lb)

continued

Poultry roasting times (continued)

Turkey (by weight)	Duration for fast roast 230°C (450°F) gas mark 8	Duration for slow roast 160°C (325°F) gas mark 3
2.70–3.60 kg (6–8 lb)	2¼–2½ hours	3–3½ hours
3.60–4.50 kg (8–10 lb)	2½–2¾ hours	3½–3¾ hours
4.50–6.30 kg (10–14 lb)	2¾–3 hours	3¾–4¼ hours
6.30–8.10 kg (14–18 lb)	3–3½ hours	4¼–4¾ hours
8.10–9.00 kg (18–20 lb)	3½–3¾ hours	4¾–5¼ hours
9.00–10.90 kg (20–24 lb)	3¾– 4¼ hours	5¼–6 hours

Game bird roasting times

Type	Oven setting	Duration
Grouse	200 °C (400 °F) gas mark 6	30–45 mins
Mallard	*See* **Duck** in **Poultry roasting times** table (p. 101)	
Partridge	200 °C (400 °F) gas mark 6	30–45 mins
Pheasant	220 °C (425 °F) gas mark 7	20 mins/454 g (1 lb)
Pigeon	220 °C (425 °F) gas mark 7	20 mins/454g (1 lb)
Quail	220 °C (425 °F) gas mark 7	20 mins

Furred game roasting times

Type	Oven setting	Duration
Hare		
• whole	200 °C (400 °F) gas mark 6	45–50 mins
• saddle	200 °C (400 °F) gas mark 6	30–35 mins
Rabbit		
• whole	200 °C (400 °F) gas mark 6	50–60 mins
Venison		
• less than 1.80 kg (4 lb)	190 °C (375 °F) gas mark 5	20 mins/454 g (1 lb)
• more than 1.80 kg (4 lb)	190 °C (375 °F) gas mark 5	15 mins/454 g (1 lb)

SEAFOOD

Types of seafood

Seafood includes both fish and shellfish. These are categorized as follows:

Fish
Flat fish
Round fish
Oily fish

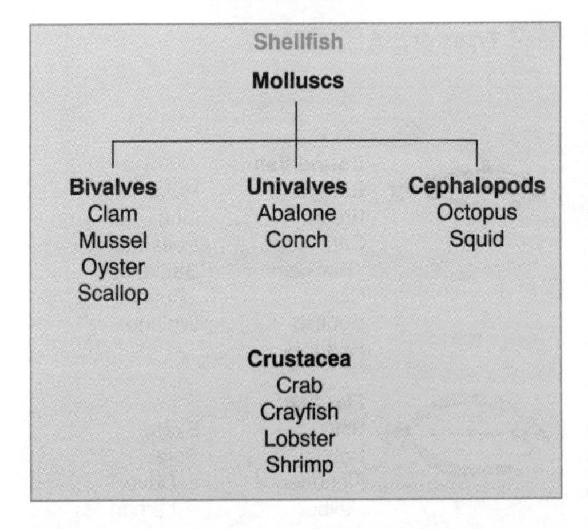

Fish can be categorized according to their oil content and their shape:

Oil content

- **White fish** Contain oil only in their liver. All come from the sea.
- **Oily fish** Contain oil distributed throughout their bodies. Most come from the sea, some are freshwater.

Shape

- **Round fish** Have near cylindrical bodies.
- **Flat fish** Have wide, flattened bodies.

Types of fish

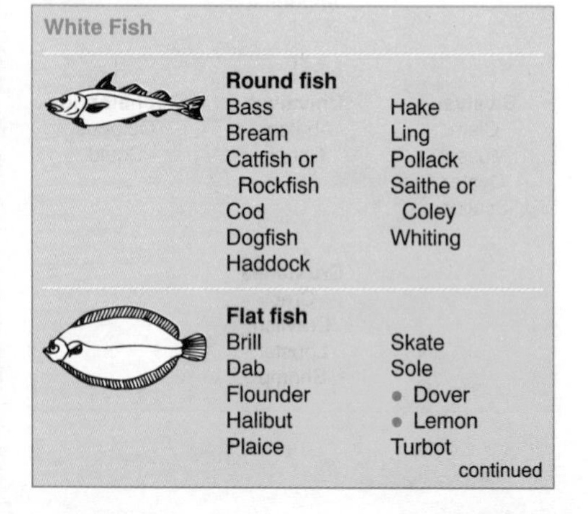

White Fish		
	Round fish	
	Bass	Hake
	Bream	Ling
	Catfish or Rockfish	Pollack
	Cod	Saithe or Coley
	Dogfish	Whiting
	Haddock	
	Flat fish	
	Brill	Skate
	Dab	Sole
	Flounder	• Dover
	Halibut	• Lemon
	Plaice	Turbot

continued

Types of fish (continued)

Oily fish		
Carp	Mullet	Trout
Eel	• Grey	• Rainbow
Herring	• Red	• River
Mackerel	Salmon	• Sea
	Sprat	

Types of shellfish

Crustacea		
Crab	Crayfish	Prawn, Dublin Bay (scampi)
Crawfish (Spring lobster)	Lobster	Shrimp
	Prawn	
Molluscs		
Clam	Oyster	Squid
Cockle	• European	Whelk
Mussel	• Pacific	Winkle
Octopus	Scallop	

Buying seafood

Tips for buying fresh fish

- Check that it is a good time of year to buy the fish you intend to use (*see* **Fish buying seasons** tables on pp. 109–110).

- For best results always buy fresh fish on the day it is to be cooked.
- Check fish for any unpleasant odour that might indicate decay. Fresh fish should be virtually odourless or smell faintly of salt water.
- Eyes should be bright and moist.
- Scales should be intact over the whole fish and should be moist and shiny.
- Flesh should be firm and moist.
- Gills should be pinky-red inside.
- When buying fillets or steaks check that the flesh is snowy white and has no yellow tinge.

Tips for buying fresh shellfish

Crustacea

- Crabs and lobsters can be purchased alive, but they are also widely available ready cooked.
- Fresh crabs and lobsters should feel heavy for their size.
- Male crabs and lobsters are a better buy than female crabs or lobsters because they tend to have larger claws and, therefore, more meat. Male lobsters can also be identified by their larger tails.

Molluscs

- Cockles, mussels and oysters must be purchased alive to ensure that they are absolutely fresh. Their shells should be clamped tightly shut, or should close immediately when tapped.
- Reject any with broken or damaged shells, and any which float in water.

Buying seasons for white fish

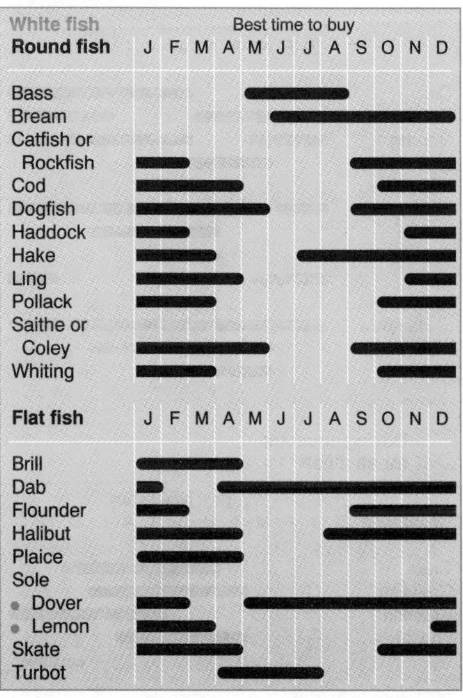

Buying seasons for oily fish

Buying seasons for shellfish

Buying seasons for shellfish (continued)

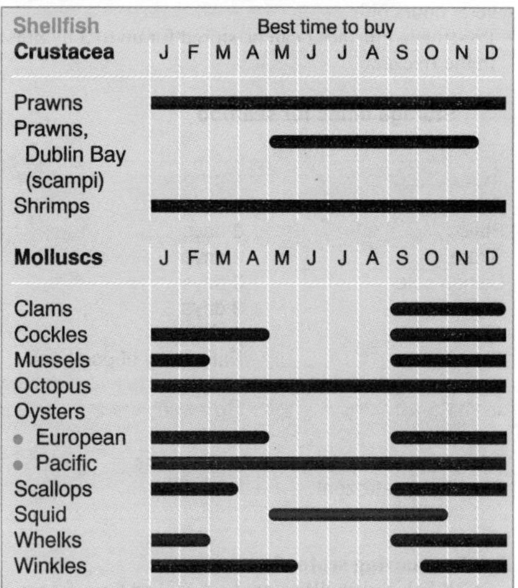

Storing seafood

Tips for storing seafood

- Molluscs should be eaten on the day of purchase; store them in the fridge until needed.
- Fish and crustacea need to be absolutely fresh when frozen; it is not safe to home freeze fish or shellfish

bought from fresh fish counters as they are likely to be several hours old.

- Pre-frozen crustacea can be stored for up to 3 months in the freezer.

Storage times for seafood

In the fridge	Duration
Plaice	3 days
Skate	3 days
Lemon sole	3 days
Smoked fish	3 days
All other fish	1–2 days
Shellfish	Eat on day of purchase
In the freezer	**Duration**
All fish	4–6 months
Shellfish (prefrozen)	3 months

Tips for thawing seafood

- Small fish and shellfish are best cooked from frozen.
- Large fish should be defrosted in the fridge for 5–6 hours.
- Fillets and steaks should be defrosted in the fridge for 3–4 hours.

Cooking seafood

Fish cooking methods and times

Baking	Temperature	Time
Thick fish	180 °C (350 °F) gas mark 4	25–30 mins
Thin fish	200 °C (400 °F) gas mark 6	20 mins
Deep frying	**Temperature**	**Time**
Fillets	190 °C (375 °F)	4–6 mins
Fish balls or cakes	200 °C (400 °F)	1–2 mins
Small whole fish	190 °C (375 °F)	3–5 mins
Steaks	180 °C (350 °F)	5–7 mins
Poaching	**Time** (after simmering begins)	
Fillets	10 mins	
Steaks	12 mins	

continued

Fish cooking methods and times (continued)

Steaming	Time
Flat fillets	12–15 mins
Thin steaks	15–20 mins
Small whole fish	15–18 mins

Shellfish cooking methods and times

Type	Method and time
Clams, cockles, mussels	Steam in 1 cm (½ in) of water until shells open
Crab	Immerse in cold water and bring slowly to the boil for 10 mins/454 g (1 lb)
Lobster	Plunge into boiling water for 20–30 mins
Prawns, shrimps	Drop into boiling water for 5 mins
Scallops	Bake at 150 °C (300 °F) gas mark 2, for 5 mins or until shells open

VEGETABLES AND FRUIT
Types of vegetables and fruit

Types of vegetables

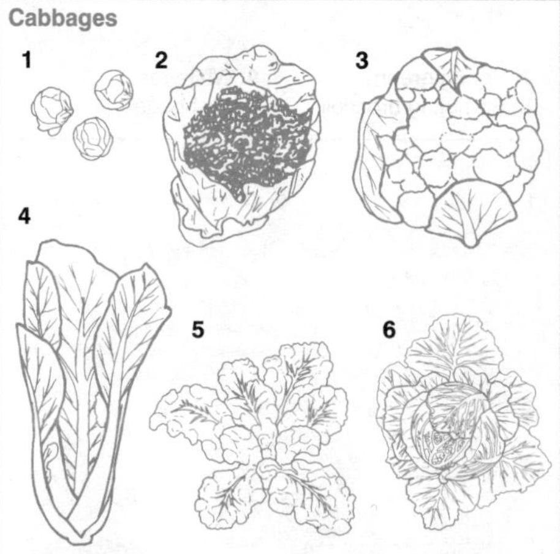

1 Brussels sprouts
2 Calabrese/Italian broccoli
3 Cauliflower
4 Chinese cabbage (Pak choi)
5 Kale
6 Savoy cabbage

continued

Types of vegetables (continued)

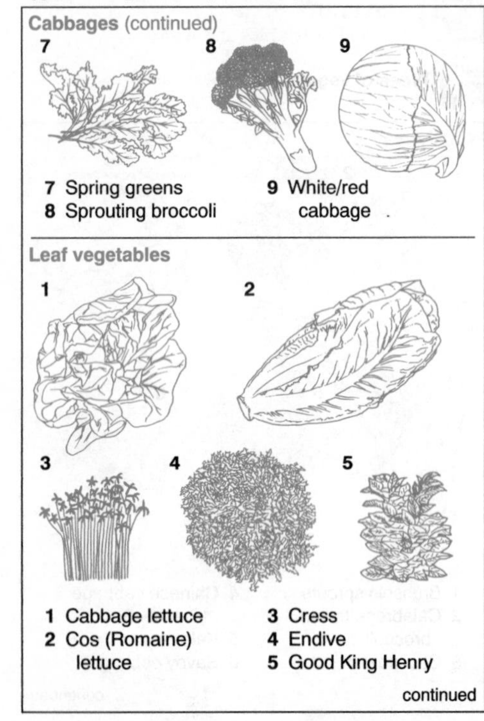

Cabbages (continued)

7 Spring greens
8 Sprouting broccoli
9 White/red cabbage

Leaf vegetables

1 Cabbage lettuce
2 Cos (Romaine) lettuce
3 Cress
4 Endive
5 Good King Henry

continued

Types of vegetables (continued)

Leaf vegetables (continued)

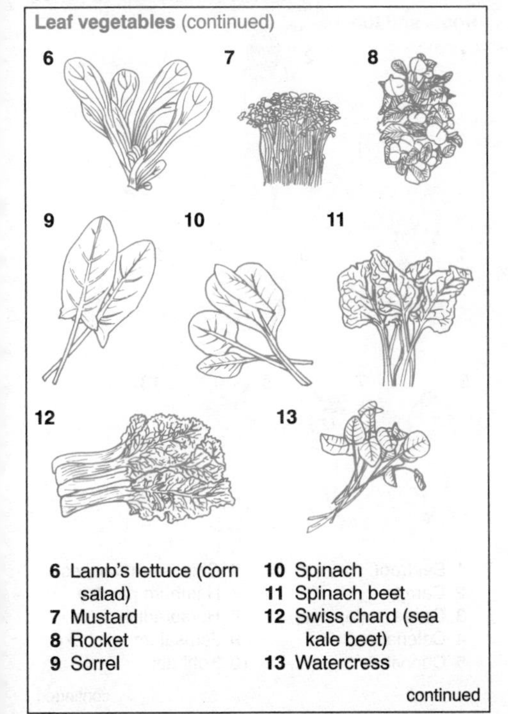

- **6** Lamb's lettuce (corn salad)
- **7** Mustard
- **8** Rocket
- **9** Sorrel
- **10** Spinach
- **11** Spinach beet
- **12** Swiss chard (sea kale beet)
- **13** Watercress

continued

Types of vegetables (continued)

Roots and tubers

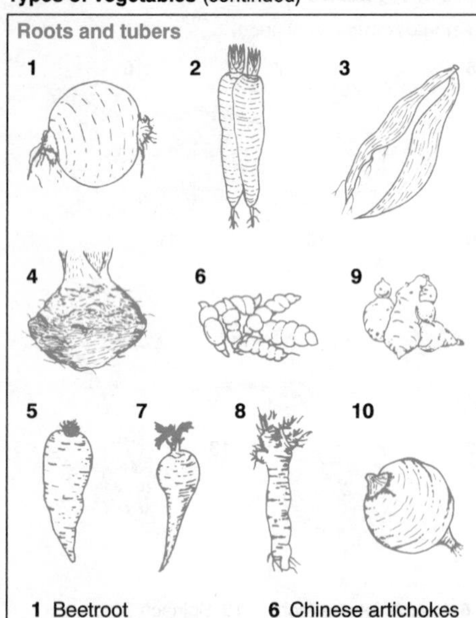

1 Beetroot
2 Carrots
3 Cassava (tapioca)
4 Celeriac
5 Chervil
6 Chinese artichokes
7 Hamburg parsley
8 Horseradish
9 Jerusalem artichoke
10 Kohlrabi

continued

Types of vegetables (continued)

Roots and tubers (continued)

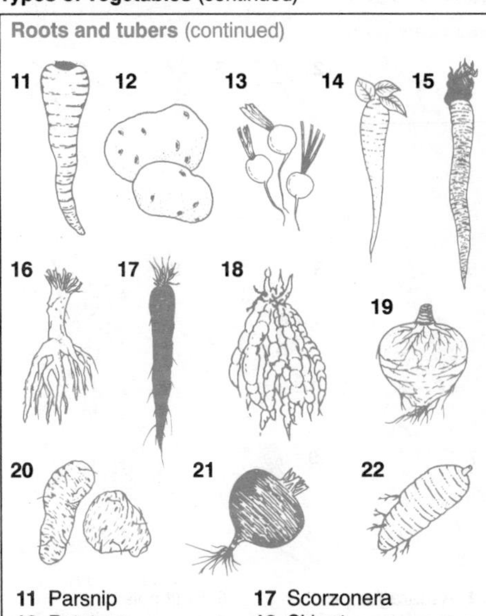

11 Parsnip
12 Potatoes
13 Radishes
14 Rampion
15 Salsify
16 Scolymus
17 Scorzonera
18 Skirret
19 Swede
20 Sweet potatoes
21 Turnip
22 Yam

continued

Types of vegetables (continued)

Seed vegetables

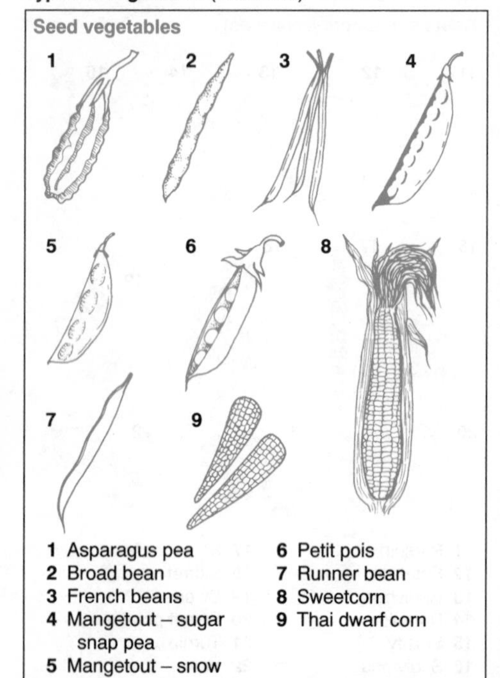

1 Asparagus pea
2 Broad bean
3 French beans
4 Mangetout – sugar snap pea
5 Mangetout – snow pea
6 Petit pois
7 Runner bean
8 Sweetcorn
9 Thai dwarf corn

continued

Types of vegetables (continued)

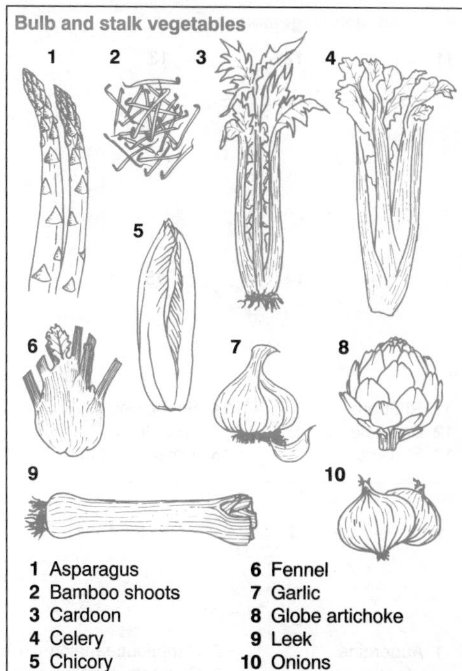

continued

Types of vegetables (continued)

Bulb and stalk vegetables (continued)

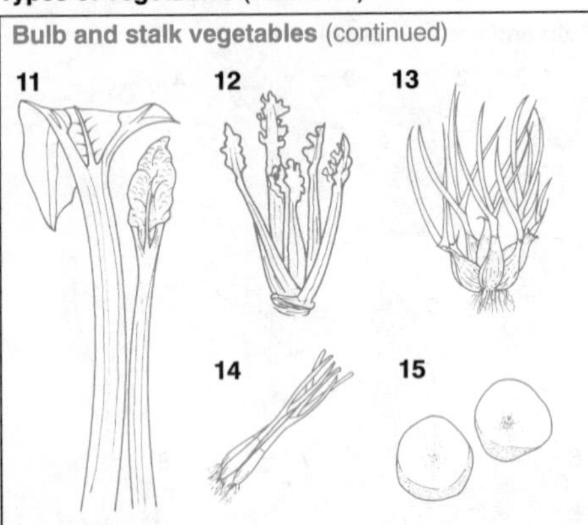

11 Rhubarb
12 Sea kale
13 Shallots
14 Spring onions (scallion)
15 Water chestnuts

Vegetable fruit

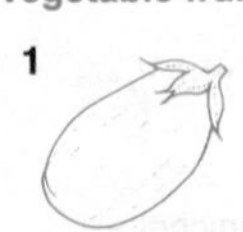

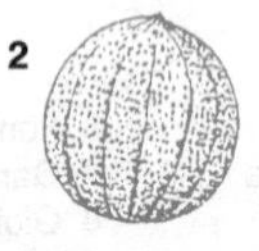

3

1 Aubergine (eggplant)
2 Cantaloupe melon
3 Charentais melon

continued

Types of vegetables (continued)

Vegetable fruit (continued)

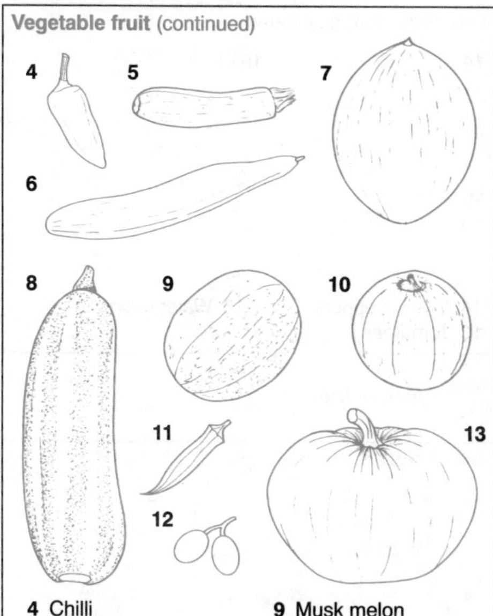

4 Chilli
5 Courgette
6 Cucumber
7 Honeydew melon
8 Marrow
9 Musk melon
10 Ogen melon
11 Okra (lady's finger)
12 Olives
13 Pumpkin

continued

Types of vegetables (continued)

Vegetable fruit (continued)

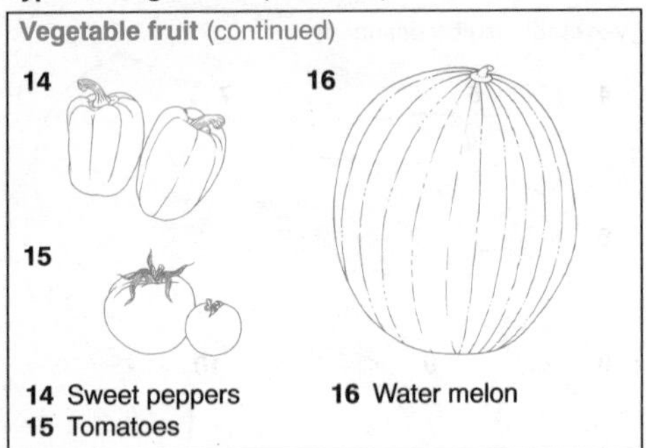

14 Sweet peppers
15 Tomatoes
16 Water melon

Types of fruit

Citrus fruit

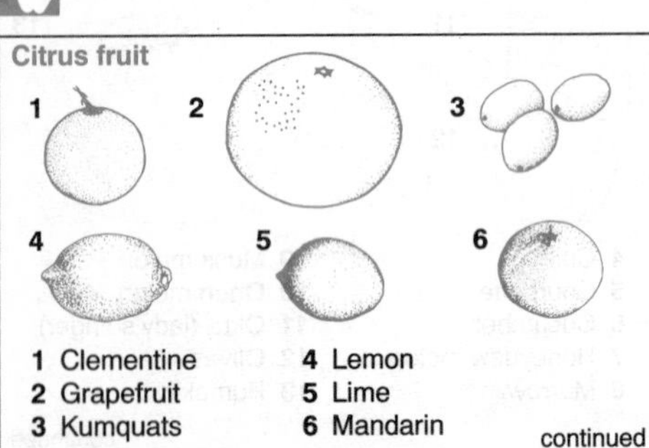

1 Clementine
2 Grapefruit
3 Kumquats
4 Lemon
5 Lime
6 Mandarin

continued

Types of fruit (continued)

Citrus fruit (continued)

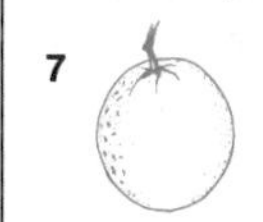
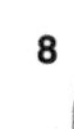
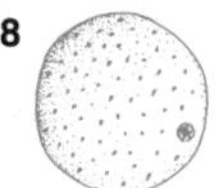
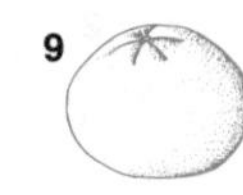
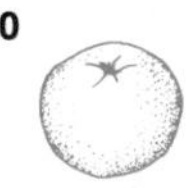
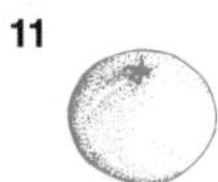
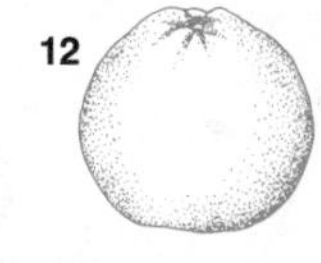

7 Naartje
8 Orange
9 Ortanique
10 Satsuma
11 Tangerine
12 Ugli

Core fruit

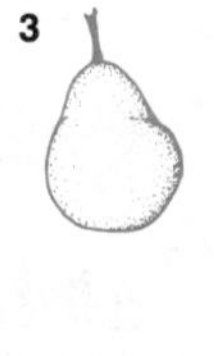

1 Apple
2 Loquat (Japanese plum)
3 Pear
4 Quince

continued

Types of fruit (continued)

Stone fruit

1 2 3 4

5 6 7

1 Apricot
2 Cherries
3 Dates
4 Greengage
5 Nectarine
6 Peach
7 Plum

Berries

1 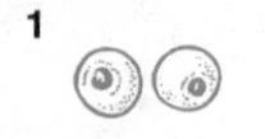 2  3 

4   5  6  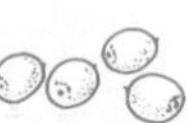

1 Bilberries
2 Blackberries
3 Blackcurrants
4 Blueberries
5 Boysenberries
6 Cranberries

continued

Types of fruit (continued)

Berries (continued)

7

8

9

10

11

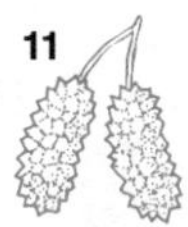

12

13

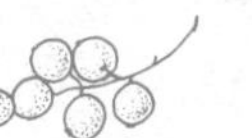

14

15

7 Dewberries
8 Gooseberries
9 Grapes
10 Loganberries
11 Mulberries
12 Raspberries
13 Redcurrants
14 Strawberry
15 Whitecurrants

Tropical fruit

1

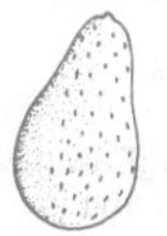

2

3

1 Avocado
2 Banana
3 Breadfruit

continued

Types of fruit (continued)

Tropical fruit (continued)

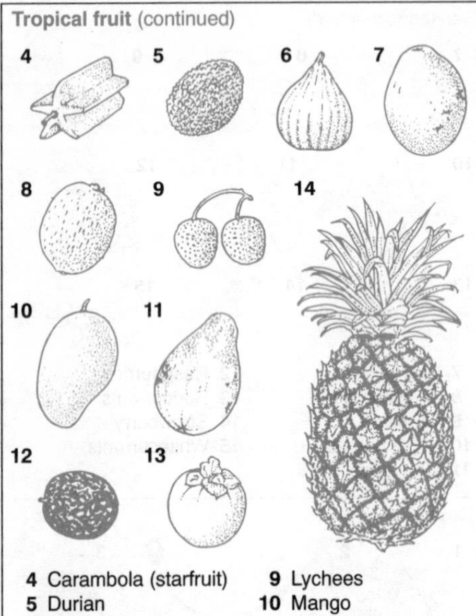

- **4** Carambola (starfruit)
- **5** Durian
- **6** Fig
- **7** Guava
- **8** Kiwi fruit (Chinese gooseberry)
- **9** Lychees
- **10** Mango
- **11** Papaya (Paw paw)
- **12** Passion fruit
- **13** Persimmon
- **14** Pineapple

continued

Types of fruit (continued)

Tropical fruit (continued)

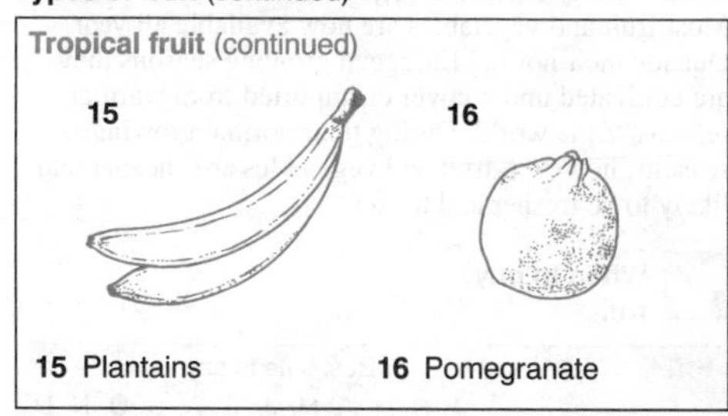

15 Plantains **16** Pomegranate

Buying vegetables and fruit

Tips for buying vegetables and fruit

- Choose fruit and vegetables that are in season – they will be fresher and better value for money than varieties that are not in season. (*See* the tables on pp. 130–1 for fruit and vegetable seasons.)
- Rather than letting the grocer choose for you or buying prepackaged fruit and vegetables, pick them out for yourself. That way you can be sure of buying the best of what is available.
- Check that fruit is firm and unbruised. Reject any fruit with a broken skin – it will rot more quickly.
- The leaves of leaf vegetables such as lettuce should be crisp and should tear cleanly.
- Buy whole items rather than ready-cut produce. Fruit and vegetables start to lose their vitamin C as soon as they are cut or damaged.

When to buy fruit and vegetables

Most fruit and vegetables are now available all year. Outside their normal European growing seasons they are cultivated under cover or imported from warmer regions of the world. During their normal growing seasons, however, fruit and vegetables are cheaper and likely to be fresher and tastier.

When to buy fruit

Fruit	J	F	M	A	M	J	J	A	S	O	N	D
	Best time to buy											
Apples									■	■	■	■
Apricots						■	■					
Bananas	■	■	■	■	■	■	■			■	■	■
Cherries						■	■					
Grapefruit	■	■	■	■							■	■
Grapes						■	■	■	■	■	■	
Lemons					■	■	■	■				
Limes						■						
Nectarines						■	■	■	■			
Oranges	■	■	■	■	■	■						■
Peaches						■	■	■	■			
Pears								■	■	■	■	
Pineapples			■	■	■	■	■	■				
Plums						■	■	■	■			
Raspberries						■	■					
Strawberries				■	■	■	■					
Tangerines	■											
Watermelons					■	■	■	■				

When to buy vegetables

Vegetable	J	F	M	A	M	J	J	A	S	O	N	D
	Best time to buy											
Asparagus					●	●						
Beans (broad)					●	●	●	●	●			
Beans (French)						●	●	●	●			
Beans (runner)							●	●	●			
Beetroot						●	●	●	●	●		
Broccoli		●	●	●	●			●	●	●	●	●
Brussels sprouts	●	●	●						●	●	●	●
Cabbage				●	●	●	●	●	●			
Carrots						●	●	●	●	●		
Cauliflower									●	●	●	
Courgettes					●	●	●	●	●			
Cucumbers				●	●	●	●					
Leeks	●	●	●						●	●	●	●
Lettuce	●	●	●	●	●	●	●	●	●	●		●
Mushrooms	●	●	●	●	●					●	●	●
Onions	●	●						●	●	●	●	●
Parsnips	●	●	●	●				●	●	●	●	●
Peas				●	●	●	●	●	●			
Potatoes (new)				●	●	●	●	●				
Potatoes (old)	●	●	●	●	●			●	●	●	●	●
Spinach	●	●					●	●	●	●	●	●
Swedes	●	●	●	●	●	●	●		●	●	●	
Sweetcorn						●	●	●	●			
Tomatoes		●	●	●	●	●	●	●	●	●		
Turnips	●	●	●					●	●	●	●	●

Storing vegetables and fruit

Freezing vegetables

Freezing is the quickest and most effective way to store vegetables for long periods. For best results some vegetables should be blanched before freezing. To blanch a vegetable place it in boiling water for a few minutes (*see* the table below) and then plunge directly into iced water. This destroys food-spoiling chemicals and seals the surface of the vegetable so that it retains nutrients and colour while frozen.

Freezing vegetables

Vegetable	Preparation	Store (months)
Artichokes (globe)	Blanch for 7 mins	12
Asparagus	Blanch for 2–3 mins	12
Beans (French)	Blanch for 2–3 mins	12
Beans (runner)	Blanch for 2 mins	6
Beetroot	Cook and skin	6
Broccoli	Break into florets then blanch for 3–4 mins	12
Brussels sprouts	Blanch for 4–6 mins	12
Cabbage	Shred then blanch for 2 mins	12
Carrots	Scrape then blanch for 5–6 mins	12

continued

Freezing vegetables (continued)

Vegetable	Preparation	Store (months)
Cauliflower	Break into florets then blanch for 3–4 mins	6
Celery	Slice then blanch for 3 mins	12
Corn (cob)	Blanch for 4–6 mins	9
Courgettes	Blanch for 1 min	12
Leeks	Slice then blanch for 1–3 mins	12
Mushrooms	Wash and fry	3
Onions	Slice then blanch for 1–2 mins	3
Parsley	Wash	6
Parsnips	Slice then blanch for 2 mins	12
Peas	Blanch for 1–2 mins	12
Potatoes (chips)	Fry for 3 mins	6
Potatoes (new)	Blanch for 4 mins	6
Spinach	Blanch for 1–2 mins	12
Tomatoes	Purée	12
Turnips	Scrape and slice then blanch for 2–3 mins	12

Freezing fruit
Packing methods

- **Dry packing (unsweetened) method** Store fruit whole, sliced, diced or puréed, in sealed freezer bags or shallow containers.
- **Sugar layering method** Place alternate layers of fruit and sugar into a large, shallow container. Shake gently to distribute sugar evenly and seal.
- **Sugar packing method** Sprinkle white granulated sugar over fruit and mix gently until it dissolves. Spoon mixture into wide-mouthed containers, leaving space for expansion, and seal.
- **Syrup method** Place fruit into a sealable container and completely cover with cold sugar syrup. Leave enough space for the syrup to expand on freezing and seal the lid.

  To make syrup for freezing:
  - **Light syrup:** dissolve 500 g (17 ½ oz) sugar, honey or corn syrup in every 1 litre (1¾ pt) of water.
  - **Heavy syrup:** dissolve 500 g (17 ½ oz) sugar, honey or corn syrup in every 500 ml (17 ½ fl oz) of water.

Note: The flesh of some fruits, such as apples, quickly turns brown when exposed to air. This process will also occur in the freezer. To prevent it, mix lemon juice or ascorbic acid into the syrup or cover vulnerable puréed fruits with ascorbic acid diluted in water (known as acidulated water).

Freezing fruit

Fruit	Preparation	Packing method
Apples	**1** Peel and slice. Blanch for 1–2 mins, **or**	Dry, sugar layer or light syrup
	2 Purée	Dry
Apricots	Purée	Light syrup
Blackberries/ loganberries/ raspberries/ strawberries	**1** Wash	Dry or sugar layer
	2 Purée	Dry
Blackcurrants/ redcurrants	Wash	Dry or sugar layer
Cherries	**1** Wash, **or**	Dry
	2 Wash and stone	Light syrup or sugar layer
Gooseberries	**1** Wash, **or**	Dry or heavy syrup
	2 Purée	Dry
Grapefruit	Peel and segment	Sugar pack or heavy syrup
Melons	Cube	Light syrup
Oranges	Peel and segment	Sugar pack or heavy syrup

continued

Freezing fruit (continued)

Fruit	Preparation	Packing method
Peaches	**1** Peel and stone, **or**	Light syrup
	2 Purée	Dry
Pineapple	Peel and slice	Sugar pack or light syrup
Plums	Peel and stone	Light syrup
Rhubarb	**1** Slice then blanch for 1 min, **or**	Sugar layer
	2 Purée	Dry

Preserving fruit

Methods for bottling fruit

- **Cold water bath method** The most thorough sterilizing process. Fruit is preserved largely intact.
- **Hot water bath method** A quicker sterilizing process which causes fruit to disintegrate a little.

Instructions for cold water bath method

- Put fruit into jars and pour in cold water or syrup until fruit is completely immersed. Make sure the jar is filled to the brim. Screw on the lid, but not so tightly that pressure cannot be released during heating.
- Immerse sealed jars completely in a pan of cold water. Place something in the bottom of the pan to prevent the jars touching the pan.
- Follow **Heating instructions** opposite.

- Lift jars out of the water while still hot and immediately seal their lids tightly. Check seals are still tight 48 hours later.

Heating instructions: cold water bath method

1 Gently raise water temperature to 54 °C (130 °F) over the course of 1 hour.

2 Continue heating at these temperatures:

Fruit	Temperature	Duration
Soft	74 °C (165 °F)	10 mins
Stone	83 °C (180 °F)	15 mins
Citrus	83 °C (180 °F)	15 mins

Instructions for hot water bath method

- Put fruit into warmed jars and pour in hot water or syrup until fruit is completely immersed. Make sure the jar is filled to the brim. Screw on the lid, but not so tightly that pressure cannot be released during heating.
- Immerse sealed jars completely in a pan of hot water. Place something in the bottom of the pan to prevent the jars touching the pan.
- Follow **Heating instructions** below.
- Lift jars out of the water while still hot and immediately seal their lids tightly. Check seals are still tight 48 hours later.

Heating instructions: hot water bath method

1 Gently raise water temperature to 87 °C (190 °F) over 25–30 minutes.

continued

Heating instructions (continued)

2 Continue heating at these temperatures:

Fruit	Temperature	Duration
Soft	74 °C (165 °F)	2 mins
Stone	83 °C (180 °F)	10 mins
Citrus	83 °C (180 °F)	10 mins

Cooking vegetables

To ensure that the maximum nutritional value is retained when boiling vegetables, use the minimum amount of water and do not cook for too long. Boiled vegetables should still be firm and crisp. Steaming is the best way to preserve the maximum goodness.

Vegetable boiling and steaming times

Type	Boiling (mins)	Steaming (mins)
Artichoke		
• globe (whole)	40–45	50–55
• Jerusalem (whole)	25–30	35–40
Asparagus (spears)	11–14	12–16
Beans		
• Broad	10–15	15–20
• French	5–10	10–15
• Runner	5–10	15–20
Beetroot (whole)	60–120	120–130

continued

Vegetable boiling and steaming times (continued)

Type	Boiling (mins)	Steaming (mins)
Broccoli (florets)	15–20	20–25
Brussels sprouts (whole)	10–15	15–20
Cabbage (shredded)	5–8	10–12
Carrots (quartered)	10–30	15–40
Cauliflower (florets)	12–15	15–25
Celeriac (sliced)	25–30	35–40
Celery (sliced)	15–20	20–30
Corn on the cob (whole)	5–10	10–15
Courgettes (sliced)	10–15	15–20
Cucumbers (diced)	10–12	20–25
Leeks (sliced)	10–12	20–25
Marrow (diced)	10–12	20–40
Parsnips (quartered)	30–40	35–40
Peas	15–20	20–25
Potatoes (quartered)		
• new	15–20	20–25
• old	20–25	25–30
Pumpkin (diced)	20–30	35–40
Radishes (whole)	10–12	20–25
Spinach (whole)	10–12	10–15
Swedes (diced)	30–40	35–40
Turnips (quartered)	25–30	30–40

NUTS AND PULSES

Types of nuts and pulses

Types of nuts

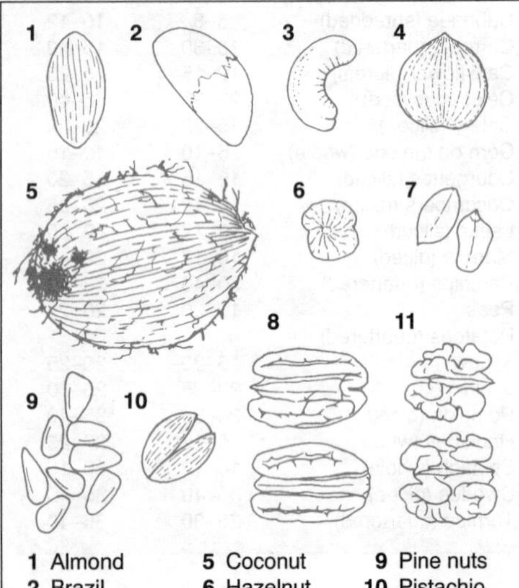

1 Almond
2 Brazil
3 Cashew
4 Chestnut
5 Coconut
6 Hazelnut
7 Peanuts
8 Pecans
9 Pine nuts
10 Pistachio
11 Walnuts

Types of pulses

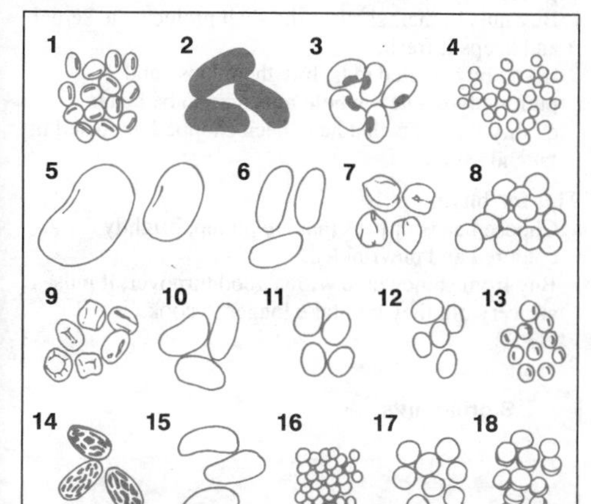

1 Adzuki beans
2 Black beans
3 Black-eyed beans
4 Brown lentils
5 Butter/lima beans
6 Cannellini beans
7 Chickpeas
8 Continental lentils
9 Dried peas
10 Flageolet beans
11 Ful medames beans
12 Haricot beans
13 Mung beans
14 Pinto beans
15 Red kidney beans
16 Red split lentils
17 Soya beans
18 Split peas (green/yellow)

Buying nuts and pulses

Tips for buying nuts

- Buy nuts in their shells – the shell protects the kernel and keeps it fresh.
- If you buy shelled nuts, buy them loose and preferably whole – whole nuts tend to be better quality than nuts that have been chopped or coated in fat and salted.

Tips for buying pulses

- Choose beans or peas that are plump, brightly coloured and unwrinkled.
- Buy from somewhere with a good turnover; if pulses are very old they will take longer to cook.

Storing nuts and pulses

Storing nuts

Kept in a cool place	Duration
Chopped nuts	4–6 weeks
Unshelled nuts	6 months

Storing pulses

Kept in cool, dry, dark conditions	Duration
In glass jars	1 month
Inside airtight containers	6 months

Cooking pulses

Soaking pulses

- Soak pulses overnight (for at least 8–12 hours) in cold water.
- Use plenty of water – pulses can absorb up to 2 or 3 times their dry volume.
- A quicker method is to boil pulses in water, simmer for 3–5 minutes and leave to stand for 1–2 hours.

Minimum boiling times for pulses

Type	Boiling time (mins)
Adzuki beans	45
Black beans	50–60
Black-eyed beans	45–50
Brown lentils	30–45
Butter/lima beans	60–90*(*see over*)
Cannellini beans	45–50
Chickpeas	60–90
Continental lentils	30–45
Dried peas	60–90
Flageolet beans	50
Ful medames beans	50
Haricot beans	50–60
Mung beans	30–45
Pinto beans	60–90

continued

Minimum boiling times for pulses (continued)

Type	Boiling time (mins)
Red kidney beans	50*
Red split lentils	15–30
Soya beans	180
Split peas (green/yellow)	40–45

Warning: Red kidney and butter/lima beans contain small amounts of a poisonous substance. These beans should be boiled hard for ten minutes in a saucepan without a lid to destroy the toxins; they can then be safely cooked as quickly or slowly as desired.

HERBS AND SPICES

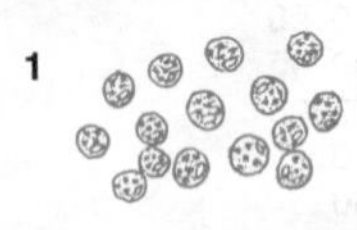

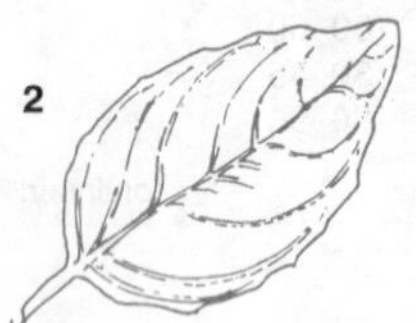

Types of herbs and spices

Allspice (1) Tastes like a combination of cloves, cinnamon and nutmeg. Grind dried berries over meats or add to fruitcake.

Basil (2) Use fresh leaves with oily fish, poultry, game birds or any recipe which uses tomatoes.

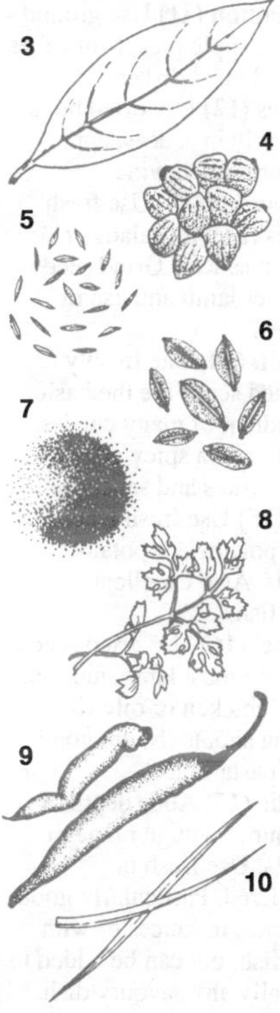

Bay (3) Use dried or fresh leaves with oily fish, pork, goose or veal.

Capers (4) Use pickled buds in sauces, pasta and meat dishes.

Caraway (5) Seeds have an aniseed taste. Use to add flavour to doughy breads and pickled vegetables.

Cardamom (6) Use seeds whole or freshly crushed with rice or lentil dishes.

Cayenne (7) A very hot pepper. Sprinkle sparingly on a wide range of foods. Good with white fish and crustacea.

Chervil (8) Use fresh leaves to garnish soups, white fish and shellfish.

Chillies (9) Use whole (fresh or dried), sliced or grated to add strong flavour to red meat dishes and salads. There are over 100 varieties, which vary greatly in strength, size and colour.

Chives (10) Leaves and flowers have a subtle onion flavour. Use fresh on salads and cooked vegetables.

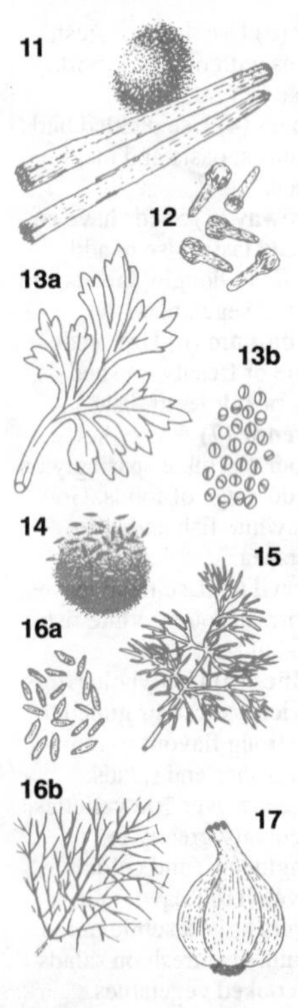

Cinnamon (11) Use ground bark in apple pies, fruit cakes and red meat dishes.

Cloves (12) Use dried buds sparingly in sauces, apple pies or mulled wine.

Coriander (13) Use fresh leaves **(a)** with salads or tomato sauces. Grind seeds **(b)** over lamb and use in curries.

Cumin (14) The freshly crushed seeds are the basic ingredient of many curries. Use to add a spicy edge to meat dishes and sauces.

Dill (15) Use fresh leaves with potatoes or potato salads. Also excellent with fish.

Fennel (16) Use dried seeds **(a)** with roast lamb, mutton, pork, chicken or oily fish. Young shoots **(b)** are good with pasta sauces.

Garlic (17) Adds depth of flavour to a huge range of dishes. Use fresh or powdered. Particularly good in stews, in sauces or with shellfish, but can be added to virtually any savoury dish.

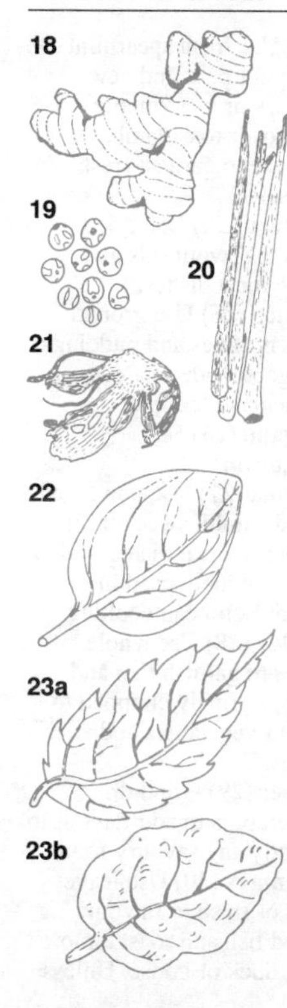

Ginger (18) Use dried or freshly chopped. Essential in Chinese, Japanese and Indian dishes. Also used in sweet and savoury European dishes.
Juniper (19) Use fresh or dried berries in marinades for game and beef.
Lemon grass (20) Use fresh or dried stalks to add a delicate lemon-like flavour. Widely used in Thai cooking.
Mace (21) Use ground and dried to enhance the flavour of roast beef or in beef casseroles. Mace is the ground outer skin of the nutmeg, to which it has a similar flavour.
Marjoram (**22**) Very similar in flavour to oregano. Use with oily fish, roast lamb and pork or with poultry and game birds.
Mint (23) There are four common varieties: spearmint (**a**), apple mint (**b**), peppermint (**c** *see over*) and pennyroyal (**d** *see over*), each with a subtly distinct

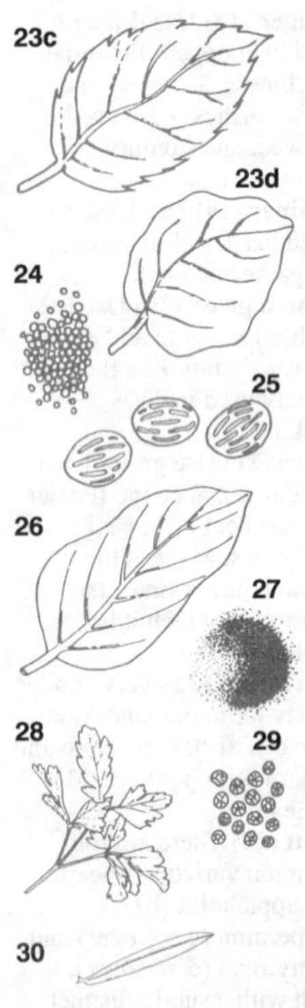

taste. Use fresh spearmint to flavour peas and new potatoes or in a vinegar sauce over roast lamb. Also use to garnish fresh fruit salads.

Mustard (24) Use dried seeds to flavour oils and strong meat dishes.

Nutmeg (25) Use ground seeds in cakes and puddings; also good with potatoes, spinach and lasagne.

Oregano (26) *See* **Marjoram**.

Paprika (27) Use powdered to add a mild, sweet chilli flavour to meat dishes and sauces. Widely used in central European cooking.

Parsley (28) Use whole leaves to garnish fish and soups, or finely chopped to flavour vegetables and sauces.

Pepper (29) Grind dried peppercorns to add flavour to virtually any savoury food.

Rosemary (30) Use leaves dried or fresh to flavour grilled fish and roast lamb, pork, duck or goose. Unless

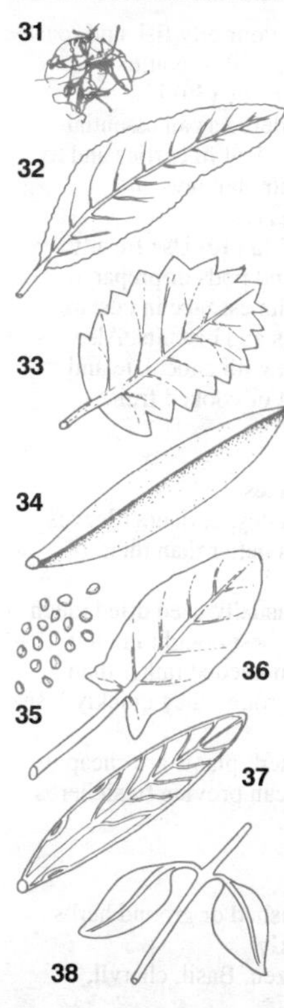

finley chopped, the spiky leaves are best removed before serving.

Saffron (31) Use a very few dried threads in baking or in rice dishes. Used in Indian dishes.

Sage (32) Use fresh or dried leaves sparingly in stuffings, or cook with liver or roast pork.

Salad burnet (33) Use fresh leaves in salads and to flavour soups.

Savory (34) Comes in two varieties: winter and summer savory. Summer savory has the more delicate flavour. Use fresh leaves to flavour salads, soups, grilled fish or egg dishes; also good with runner beans.

Sesame (35) Use whole seeds to add a nutty topping to plain breads and rolls.

Sorrel (36) Use fresh leaves in sauces to accompany fish.

Tarragon (37) Use fresh leaves to enhance the flavour of chicken. Also good with oily fish and omelettes.

Thyme (38) Use fresh leaves

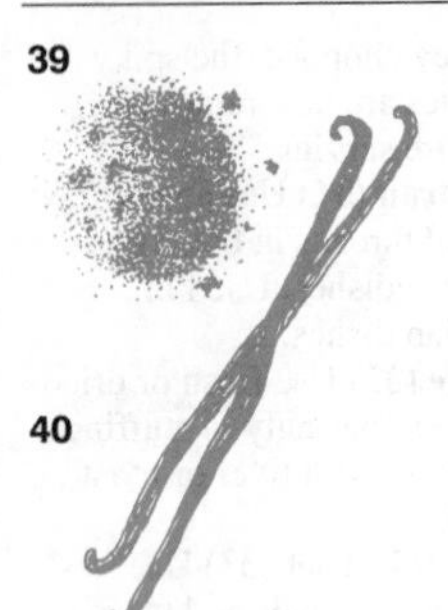

to flavour oily fish and roast pork, veal or poultry.

Turmeric (39) Use powdered as an essential ingredient in curries and to colour chutneys and preserves.

Vanilla (40) Use freshly ground pods or prepared vanilla essence in custard, cakes and biscuits. Also good with chocolate and fresh or cooked fruit.

Buying herbs and spices

Tips for buying herbs and spices

- Fresh herbs such as mint, parsley, coriander leaves and chives are almost always better than their dried versions.
- Herbs and spices which are usually used dried (such as pepper and cinnamon) are best bought in their whole form and ground when needed rather than bought ready ground. Once ground they quickly lose their flavour.
- Many varieties of common herb plants are cheap to buy and easy to grow. They can provide fresh herbs all year round.

Storing herbs and spices

- Store dried herbs whole. Crushed or ground herbs lose their flavour more quickly.
- Many fresh herbs can be frozen. Basil, chervil,

chives, dill, fennel, marjoram, mint, parsley, rosemary, sage, tarragon and thyme respond well to freezing and retain a full, fresh flavour when defrosted. Pack in plastic bags for freezing.

- Store herbs out of direct light and in a cool place. Heat and light can cause their delicate oils to evaporate and flavour to be lost.

Cooking with herbs and spices

- Dried or powdered herbs and spices are much more concentrated than the fresh or unground variety. Use about a third of the quantity of the fresh version.

DAIRY PRODUCTS

Types of dairy milk

Condensed milk Has been heated to evaporate about 50 per cent of its water content. It is not sterilized and will spoil quickly if not refrigerated.

Evaporated milk Has been heated to evaporate about 60 per cent of its water content and then sterilized. It will keep almost indefinitely in its sealed container.

Homogenized milk Has been forced through tiny holes under high pressure to break up its fat globules and distribute them evenly throughout.

Pasteurized milk Has been heated to kill bacteria. Nearly all milk that is sold has been pasteurized. There are several methods:

- **HTST (High-Temperature Short-Time)**
  Heated to 72 °C for 15 seconds
- **Batch method**
  Heated to 63 °C for 30 seconds

- **Ultrapasteurization**
  Heated to 138 °C for 2 seconds
- **UHT (Ultra Heat Treatment)** or **sterilization**
  Heated to 149 °C for 6–9 seconds

Powdered milk Has had all its water content removed. Powdered milk is available in whole milk and skimmed milk varieties.
Raw milk Comes directly from the producer and has undergone no treatment other than cooling. It is rarely sold to the public.
Semi-skimmed/half fat milk Has had about half of its fat content removed.
Skimmed milk Has had almost all of its fat content removed (contains about 0.1 per cent fat).
Whole milk Has had none of its fat content removed. It may be homogenized, pasteurized or powdered.

Milk equivalents
Most recipes assume that you will be using full fat, pasteurized milk. The table below shows how to make its equivalent using other types of milk.

Milk equivalents

1 cup of full fat milk is equal to:
• ½ cup of evaporated milk + ½ cup of water
• ½ cup of condensed milk + ½ cup of water
• 4 tablespoons of powdered whole milk + 1 cup of water
• 4 tablespoons of powdered skimmed milk + 2 tablespoons of butter + 1 cup of water

Types of egg

Hens' eggs By far the most common kind used in cooking, although other kinds such as duck and quail eggs can also be purchased.
Free range eggs Most hens' eggs are laid by battery hens, which are kept under conditions that some people feel are cruel and unhealthy. Free range eggs are laid by hens that live a more natural life.
Powdered egg Eggs from which all the liquid has been removed. Used mainly for large-scale catering or in circumstances where fresh eggs cannot be stored.
White and brown shelled eggs Laid by different breeds of chicken but taste identical and have the same nutritional content.

Buying eggs

Different sizes of eggs are best used for different kinds of cooking: most recipes stipulate which size of egg to use. If no size is given assume 'take one egg' means a size 3 egg (the most common size of egg sold).

Egg sizes

Egg size	Weight	Egg size	Weight
1	70 g or more	5	50–54 g
2	65–69 g	6	45–49 g
3	60–64 g	7	less than 45 g
4	55–59 g		

Egg sizes and uses

Sizes	Use for
1–3	Boiling
3–4	Frying and poaching
5–7	Cake-making and scrambling

Boiling eggs

Soft-boiled eggs Bring a pan of water to the boil and then place the eggs in the water. Continue boiling for 4–5 minutes.
Medium-boiled eggs Put the eggs in a saucepan of cold water. Bring the water to the boil and then immediately remove the pan from the heat. Cover the pan with a lid and leave to stand for 5–7 minutes.
Hard-boiled eggs Place the eggs in cold water, bring to the boil and boil for 10 minutes. Then plunge the eggs into cold water to prevent further cooking and to loosen the shell for easier peeling.

Types of cheese

Cheese is essentially solidified milk. The various processes used to make cheese create several distinct groups of cheese.

Types of cheese

Fresh cheese	Made with cream. These cheeses are very soft and can be spread easily. They are not matured. Examples include Boursin, Fromage frais and Mascarpone.
Soft cheese	Whey is drained without pressure. These cheeses are soft and stick to a knife. They are matured quickly. Examples include Brie, Caerphilly, Camembert and Mozzarella.
Semi-hard cheese	Whey is drained under a little pressure. These cheeses are firm but slice easily. They are matured slowly. Examples include Appenzell, Gorgonzola, Gouda, Jarlsberg, Leicester, Port-Salut, Roquefort, Stilton and Wensleydale.
Hard cheese	Whey is squeezed out under high pressure. These cheeses are hard to very hard: they are matured very slowly. The hardest can be difficult to cut but ideal for grating. Examples include Cheddar, Cheshire, Double Gloucester, Emmental, Gruyère and Parmesan.

continued

Types of cheese (continued)

Vegetarian cheese	Animal rennet is not used to curdle the milk. Examples include Feta and Ricotta.
Lean cheese	Made from skimmed milk. Examples include Blue Vinny, Elbo and Leiden.
Processed cheese	Made by mixing and heating several natural cheeses with chemicals called emulsifiers. The result is a soft textured cheese which keeps well. Cheese spreads have added milk or cream.

Storing dairy products

Tips for refrigerating dairy products

- **Butter and margarine** Should be kept wrapped to prevent it absorbing smells from other foods.
- **Cheese** Should be tightly wrapped to prevent it losing moisture. Cheese absorbs smells easily, so keep it away from strongly flavoured foods.
- **Eggs, fresh** Do not wash eggs before storing; their shells have a natural protective film which helps to keep them fresh. Store eggs pointed end downward so that the yolk, which deteriorates quickest, is completely covered by the white. Eggs absorb smells easily, so keep them away from strongly flavoured foods.

- **Eggs, broken** Separate yolks from whites and store apart. Keep yolks immersed in water; store whites in a sealed container.
- **Milk** Pasteurized milk keeps for longer than raw milk but will spoil quickly if not refrigerated. Sterilized or UHT milk can be kept for 6 months unrefrigerated as long as it remains sealed in its original container.

See table on p. 158 for fridge storing times.

Tips for freezing dairy products

- **Butter and margarine** Should be stored wrapped or in a container. Unsalted butter keeps better than salted.
- **Cheese** Hard cheese tends to dry out quickly when defrosted, so pack in portions small enough to be used quickly. Softer cheeses freeze well.
- **Cream and cream cheese** Will separate but can be used in cooking after defrosting and passing through a blender.
- **Eggs** Break eggs into a bowl and beat together lightly before freezing. Or separate yolks from whites and freeze separately. Yolks will coagulate if frozen on their own unless mixed with salt, honey, sugar or corn syrup. For every six yolks add 1 tablespoon of salt or 2 tablespoons of honey, sugar or corn syrup.
- **Whipping cream** Can be frozen in liquid form or, for best results, can be whipped and sweetened before freezing.

See table on p. 158 for freezer storing times.

Storage times for dairy products

In the fridge	Duration
Butter	6–8 weeks
Cheese	
• fresh	4–6 days
• hard (opened)	1–2 weeks
• hard (vacuum sealed)	3 weeks
• soft	2–3 days
Cream	2–3 days
Eggs (whole)	4–5 weeks
Eggs (yolks and whites)	3 days
Margarine	3–4 weeks
Milk (pasteurized)	2–3 days
Yoghurt	2–3 days

In the freezer	Duration
Butter	8–9 months
Cheese (hard)	6 months
Eggs	
• whites	6 months
• whole (beaten)	6 months
• yolks	6 months
Ice cream	1–2 months
Margarine	6 months
Milk (pasteurized)	6 weeks
Whipped cream	2–4 months
Yoghurt	6 weeks

MISCELLANEOUS FOODS

Types of bread

Yeast bread Bread in which yeast has been used to leaven (raise) the dough. This is the most common form of bread. Most yeast breads are baked in tins; some, e.g. rye bread and French baguettes, are baked on a flat tray. Most bread rolls are yeast breads. Common types of yeast bread include:

- **White bread** Made with flour from which the germ (embryo of a new plant) and bran (fibrous outer casing of the grain) have been removed by milling.
- **Brown bread** Made with flour which retains some or all of the germ and bran. Some brown bread is simply white bread coloured with caramel.
- **Wholemeal/wholewheat bread** Made with flour which retains all parts of the wheat grain.
- **Stoneground bread** Modern mills use large metal rollers moving at high speed to grind grain. These generate so much heat that some of the enzymes and vitamins in wholemeal flour are destroyed. Stoneground flour is made using traditional mill-stones which do not damage the nutrients derived from whole grains.

Quick bread Ingredients other than yeast (e.g. baking powder) are used to leaven the dough. Examples include soda bread, bridge rolls and muffins.

Flat bread Also called unleavened bread because no leavening agents are added to the dough. It is baked on a flat tray. Examples include tortillas, chapatti and pitta bread. (Nan bread is slightly leavened bread.)

Types of flour

Arrowroot flour A very fine flour used to thicken liquids and sauces.
Barley flour Used in bread-making, but usually combined with a larger quantity of wheat flour.
Buckwheat flour Used to make pancakes, blinis and similar unleavened products.
Cornflour A fine flour made from maize. Used to thicken liquids and sauces.
Maize flour Has a yellow colour and is coarser than other flours. Used to make tortillas and a great variety of traditional staple foods around the world.
Potato flour Used to thicken sauces and, especially, soups and stews.
Rice flour A very fine flour used to thicken sauces and to absorb surplus moisture from the surface of cooked foods.
Rye flour Used to make rye bread.
Wheat flour Used to make bread and pasta and for baking. Some varieties of wheat are rich in an elastic substance called gluten which is very good at retaining bubbles created by leavening agents. Flours made from these varieties are known as *strong flours* and are essential in bread-making. Flour which does not contain gluten or has a form of gluten which does not retain bubbles well is known as *weak flour*. Common types of wheat flour include:

- **Durum flour** An Italian wheat flour rich in gluten which is widely used to make pasta. The Italian term *semolino di gran duro* on pasta packaging indicates that it has been made using durum wheat flour.

- **Plain flour** Usually a blend of high and low gluten flours with vitamins, thiamin and niacin added. Used for general purpose home baking.
- **Self-raising flour** A plain flour with leavening agents (e.g. bicarbonate of soda) already added. Used as a general purpose flour for home-baked cakes and scones.
- **Wholemeal/wholewheat flour** The flour of wheat from which the germ and bran have not been removed during milling. Usually a blend containing a high proportion of gluten-rich flours. Ideal for making bread.

Types of oil

Oils are obtained from seeds, beans and nuts. They are a major source of energy and, when unrefined, of vitamins and minerals, especially vitamin E (*see* **Section 5** pp. 200–7 for more information on vitamins). Different types of oil contain different proportions of saturated and unsaturated fats. Unsaturated fats are considered to be less harmful to health than saturated fats. *See* **Chapter 5** pp. 196–9 for the nutritional values of all types of fat. *See* p. 199 for a table giving the fat composition of various oils.

Oil processing

- **Cold-pressed oil (unrefined)** Extracted using traditional hydraulic presses. The extracted oil is expensive but of high quality, with plenty of nutrients and flavour. No preservatives are added so the oil must be refrigerated when opened. Refrigeration makes it semi-solid, but at room temperature it returns to liquid form. This oil is best used raw, e.g. as a salad dressing.

- **Semi-refined oil** Extracted under greater pressure than cold-pressed oil and at high temperatures. Nutrient content is lower than unrefined oil.
- **Refined oil** Sometimes called 'pure', this oil loses much of its natural colour and odour through processing. Preservatives are added to stop the oil going rancid. Vitamins lost in processing are replaced. It is the cheapest oil to buy.

Some common oils

- **Corn (maize) oil** Popular as a cooking oil, cheap to buy and high in polyunsaturates, but has little flavour. Its high smoking-point makes it suitable for stir-frying and deep-frying.
- **Olive oil** The finest version, extra-virgin olive oil, is a cold-pressed oil that is extracted from the first pressing of olives. It is the most fragrant and flavourful of the olive oils and is used for salads and other uncooked dishes. Cruder versions (i.e. oil from second and later pressings made under heat) are suitable for cooking.
- **Peanut oil** A pleasant, mild taste. It can be heated to high temperatures and is suitable for stir-frying and deep-frying.
- **Safflower oil** Extracted from the seed of the safflower plant by hydraulic or chemical means. It is low in saturated fats, has a mild flavour and is suitable as a salad oil or for deep-frying.
- **Sesame oil** There are two main types. The first, made from roasted sesame seeds, is a flavourful and

aromatic brown oil; it is mainly used as a dressing. The second type, made from unroasted sesame seeds, is lighter and has a slightly sweet smell. It is popular as a frying oil and for baking (it does not turn rancid so baked foods last longer).

- **Soya oil** Made from soya beans. It is high in polyunsaturates, strong tasting and relatively cheap to buy. Good for stir-frys.
- **Sunflower oil** Very popular all-purpose oil, high in polyunsaturates and relatively cheap to buy.

Cooking with oil

Above certain temperatures cooking oils begin to 'burn': they emit smoke and impart an unpleasant, acrid taste to foods. The higher the smoking point of an oil the better suited it is to deep-frying.

Smoking temperatures for common oils

Oil	Smoking temperature
Corn (maize) oil	210 °C (410 °F)
Olive oil	210 °C (410 °F)
Peanut oil	230 °C (450 °F)
Safflower oil	230 °C (450 °F)
Sesame oil	210 °C (410 °F)
Soya oil	230 °C (450 °F)
Sunflower oil	200 °C (390 °F)

Types of pasta

Pasta is available in fresh or dried forms. Dried pasta should not be considered inferior to fresh; traditional Italian recipes use both in different ways. Pasta is categorized according to its shape. Some of the types of dried pasta available are shown below.

Types of pasta

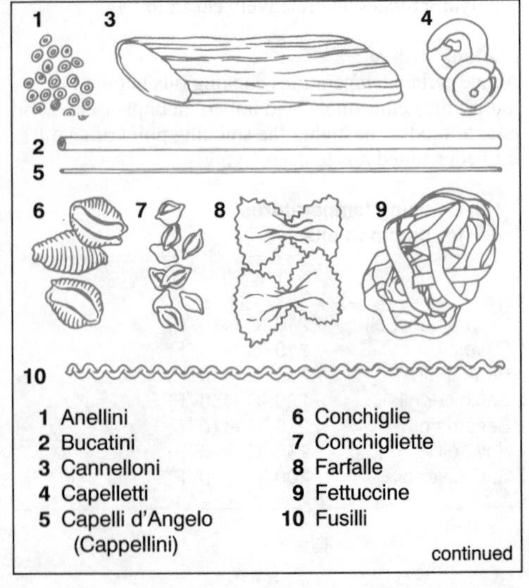

Types of pasta (continued)

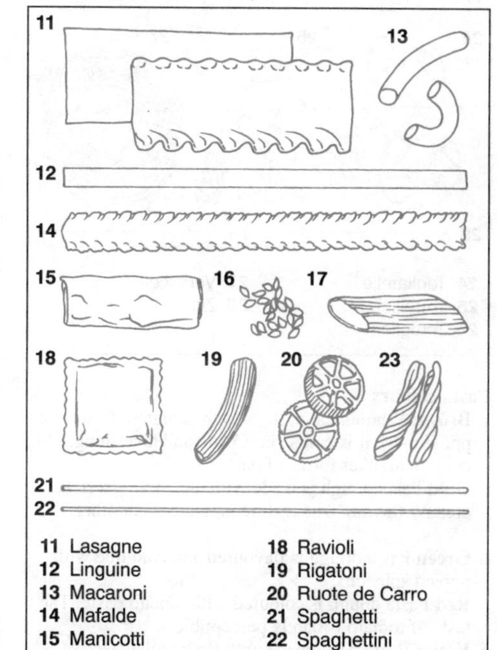

11 Lasagne
12 Linguine
13 Macaroni
14 Mafalde
15 Manicotti
16 Orzo
17 Penne Rigate
18 Ravioli
19 Rigatoni
20 Ruote de Carro
21 Spaghetti
22 Spaghettini
23 Spiedini

continued

Types of pasta (continued)

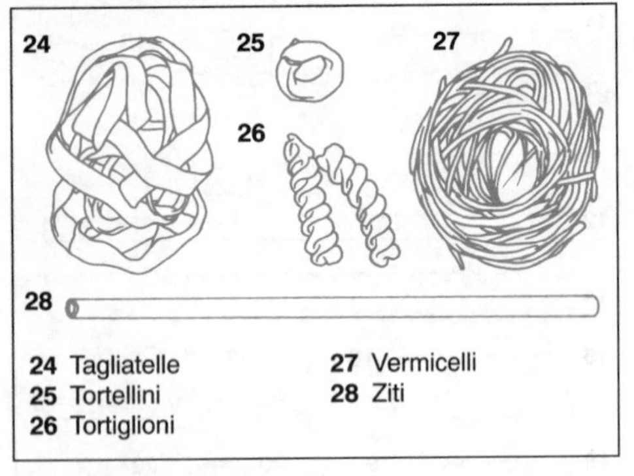

24 Tagliatelle
25 Tortellini
26 Tortiglioni
27 Vermicelli
28 Ziti

Pasta colours

- **Brown** Wholemeal pasta, which is high in fibre (see pp. 195–6). It is coarse in texture and takes longer to cook than other forms of pasta.
- **Gold** Pasta dough is made with egg, giving a rich, creamy flavour. The texture is lighter than other forms.
- **Green** Pasta dough is flavoured and coloured with puréed spinach.
- **Red** Pasta dough is coloured with tomato paste. The taste of tomato is barely perceptible.
- **White** Basic pasta made with flour and water.

Cooking pasta

Fresh pasta takes less time to cook than dried pasta. A very fine fresh pasta may be cooked in one minute; an average dried spaghetti usually takes about 7 minutes. The best way to know when pasta is done is to try a piece. Properly cooked pasta should feel firm in the centre (but not crunchy) when bitten. Pasta which has been boiled for too long begins to disintegrate and becomes very sticky. The Italian term *al dente*, which means 'to the tooth', is used to describe pasta which has been properly cooked.

Types of rice

Grain lengths

- **Long grain rice** Has long, slender grains which remain firm and separate well after cooking. It is used for main dishes, salads and soups. Basmati rice is an example of a long grain rice.
- **Medium grain rice** Has short, plump grains which tend to become soft and sticky during cooking. It is used for stuffings and croquettes. Risotto rice is an example of a medium grain rice.
- **Short grain rice** Has grains that are almost spherical and which become very sticky during cooking. It is used for making rice moulds and puddings.

Rice processing

- **Brown or unpolished rice** Retains the bran (fibrous outer casing) and germ (seed) which are removed from white rice. It has a higher nutritional value than white rice but the grains are less soft when cooked.
- **Instant or precooked rice** Has been fully cooked

and then dehydrated. It needs a short soak in hot water to prepare it before cooking.
- **Parboiled or converted rice** Has been soaked, steamed and dried before milling. It needs less cooking than ordinary rice and retains more of its nutritional content as a result.
- **White or polished rice** The bran and germ seed in brown rice is removed in processing.

Other grains
- **Wild rice** Comes from wild grasses that are similar to the ancestors of modern, commercial rice plants. It has a strong and distinctive flavour, but is much more expensive than ordinary rice.

Cooking rice

Tips for cooking rice
- Hold rice in a strainer and pour lots of cold water over it. This washes away starch and prevents the rice from becoming sticky during cooking.
- Do not overestimate the amount needed. Rice absorbs a lot of water during cooking and can treble in volume. Allow about 85–110 g (3–4 oz) per person.
- Mix a small knob of butter or a little vegetable oil into cooked rice to prevent rice grains sticking together as they cool.

Rice cooking methods
- **Boiling** Bring water to the boil and then add the rice and a little salt. Bring back to the boil and boil hard for 12 minutes.

- Use approximately 500 ml (1 pt) of water plus one teaspoon of salt per 50 g (2 oz) of rice.

- **Absorption method** Bring water to the boil and then add the rice and a little salt. When the water boils again cover immediately with a cloth and the pan lid. Place a weight on the lid to prevent steam escaping and continue boiling for 15 minutes. All the water will be absorbed by the rice.
  - Use twice as much water as rice plus one teaspoon of salt per 50 g (2 oz) of rice.

Types of sweeteners

Artificial sweeteners Man-made chemical compounds have been developed which are are much sweeter than sucrose but do not have any nutritional value. They are used to sweeten foods without adding calories. (*See* pp. 228–45 for more on additives).

Carob powder Made from the sugary pod of a Mediterranean tree. It is sweeter than cocoa but contains no caffeine, has a lower fat content and contains some vitamins. Makes cakes and biscuits a dark brown colour.

Fruit juice concentrates High in vitamins and minerals. A healthy alternative to sugar for sweetening cakes, pastries, fruit salads, sauces and cereals.

Golden syrup/Molasses/Treacle All are made from the brown liquid left over after refined sugar has been crystalized. Used to add richness to foods such as fruit breads and ginger cakes.

Honey Derived from nectar. Honey is much sweeter than sugar; if substituting in a recipe use only half as much honey. Pure honey is the healthy alternative: it undergoes less processing and refinement than blended honey, which may contain syrups and other additives.

Liquid glucose A specialized ingredient containing sugars other than sucrose. It is not as sweet as granulated sugar. Used to give a glossy appearance to semi-liquid sugar fillings or fondants and to prevent them from crystallizing.

Maple syrup A sweet syrup made from the sap of the sugar maple tree. Contains some minerals, especially calcium.

Molasses *See* Golden syrup.

Raw sugar The product derived from sugar cane and sugar beet before refining. It is between 97 and 99 per cent pure sucrose. Raw sugar is brown in colour with large, uneven crystals which tend to clump together easily. Rarely used in cooking because it is difficult to dissolve and gives food a coarse texture.

Refined sugar Processed and purified from raw sugar until it is almost 100 per cent pure sucrose. It is sold in a variety of crystalized forms:

- **Granulated sugar** The most common form of refined sugar. It is pure white and has medium sized crystals. Can be used in all kinds of cooking.
- **Caster sugar** Granulated sugar which has been lightly crushed. It dissolves more easily than granulated sugar and gives a smoother texture when used in foods.
- **Icing sugar** Granulated sugar which has been crushed to a very fine powder. It dissolves very easily and is used to make smooth pastes for icings and sweets.

- **Soft brown sugar** Granulated sugar which has been coloured with molasses or soft raw brown sugar such as Muscovado sugar. Its dark colour and rich flavour is best suited to fruit cakes.
- **Demerara sugar** A soft brown sugar from the West Indies.

Treacle *See* Golden syrup.
Vanilla sugar Granulated sugar which has been flavoured with vanilla essence or whole vanilla pods. Used to give a subtle vanilla flavour to sugary foods.

Types of vegetarian alternatives

Artificial meat substitutes

These are processed to give the taste and texture of meat. They are high in protein and low in fat. Types include:

- **Mycoprotein** Made from fungal microorganisms.
- **Texturized vegetable protein** Made from soya beans.

Dairy milk substitute

- **Soya milk** Made from soya beans. Used especially in puddings and custards.

Egg substitutes

- **Soya flour** Made from soya beans. Can be used to enrich pastry or bread dough.
  - To enrich pastry: mix 1–2 tablespoons of soya flour with every 225 g (8 oz) of wheat flour.
  - To enrich bread dough: mix 50 g (2 oz) of soya flour with every 450 g (1 lb) of wheat flour.
- **Tahini paste** Made from sesame seeds. Can be used as a binding agent.

- To bind a nut roast: instead of 2 eggs add 30 ml (2 tbsp) tahini paste plus extra stock or water.

Other vegetarian alternatives

Foods traditional to Far Eastern cuisine that are a good source of protein and other nutrients but low in fat include:

- **Miso paste** Made from fermented soya beans. All misos have a fairly high salt content. Usually added as a flavouring at the end of cooking.
- **Tofu** Unfermented soya bean curd. Used in Chinese and Japanese cooking for marinating and stir-frying, and in dressings, sauces and puddings. There are two types:
  - **Silken tofu** The softest form, with the consistency of firm junket. Used in dips, dressings, soups and sauces.
  - **Firm tofu** The hard-pressed version, with a dense texture like hard cheese and moulded into solid cakes. Used in stir-fries and for braising and poaching.

Buying and storing miscellaneous foods

Tips for buying tinned foods

- Do not buy tins which have been dented, especially if the dent is near the seam – the blow may have broken the airtight seal.
- Do not buy tins which have signs of rust – the airtight seal may have been broken by the corrosion.
- Do not buy tins which are bulging at the ends; this is a sign that the food inside has begun to decay and is giving off decomposition gases.

Tips for storing miscellaneous foods

- Do not keep foods in tins once they are opened. The presence of air will cause the metal lining to dissolve into the food.
- Store tins in a dry, cool atmosphere to prevent corrosion.
- Do not seal flour in an airtight container; water contained in the flour will make it go mouldy. Use a container which allows air to circulate.
- Store biscuits in an airtight container to prevent them from becoming stale.
- Many foods contain preservatives which may allow them to be kept for longer than indicated in the table below. For best results follow the *Best before* date on the food package.
- Store vegetable oil away from heat and light – light encourages decomposition and produces free radicals, which are associated with ageing and cell breakdown (*see* pp. 200–1).

Storage times for miscellaneous foods

In the larder	Duration
Biscuits	
• opened	7–10 days
• unopened	3–4 months
Cakes	
• fruit	10–12 months
• sponge	3–4 days

continued

Storage times for miscellaneous foods (continued)

In the larder	Duration
Flour	
• plain	10–12 months
• self raising	10 months
• wholemeal	6 months
• stoneground	3 months
Honey	18 months
Jam (unopened)	12 months
Pasta (dry)	10–12 months
Rice	10–12 months
Salad dressings (sealed)	8 months
Sugars	18 months
Syrups	12 months
Tofu, silken (sealed)	6 months
Vegetable oils (sealed)	
• cold-pressed oils	1–2 months
• refined oils	12 months
• semi-refined oils	3 months

In the fridge	Duration
Jams (opened)	2–3 weeks
Miso (sealed)	12 months
Salad dressings (opened)	1–2 months
Syrups (opened)	2–3 weeks
Tofu (fresh, in water which is changed daily)	5 days

continued

Storage times for miscellaneous foods (continued)

In the fridge	Duration
Tofu (unopened vacuum pack)	3–4 weeks
In the freezer	**Duration**
Breads	1 month
Cakes	4 months
Pastry (baked)	3 months
Pastry (unbaked)	6 months
Soups/stocks	4 months

ALCOHOLIC DRINK

Types of alcoholic drink

Ales and Beers Made with fermented barley malt and flavoured with a wide variety of ingredients. Examples are bitter, lager and stout.
Ciders Made with fermented apples. Examples are scrumpy and dry cider.
Fortified wines Made by adding spirits to wine. Examples are port and sherry.
Liqueurs Made by adding flavourings (e.g. fruit juices) to brandy, gin or other spirits. Examples are Benedictine, Cointreau and Drambuie.
Spirits Made by distilling fermented grain malts or fruit juices. Flavoured with a wide variety of ingredients.

Examples are whisky, brandy (distilled wine), vodka and rum.

Wines Usually made with fermented grapes, although wine can be made with virtually any juicy, sugar-rich fruit. The main types of wine are:

- **Red wine** Made from black grapes. Its deep red colour comes from the skins of the grapes, which are added to the juice during fermentation.
- **White wine** Can be made from black or white grapes since the skins are removed before fermentation.
- **Rosé wine** Made from black grapes. The skins are retained for part of the fermenting process; only a little of their colour is transferred, producing a light pinkish wine.
- **Blush wine** A very pale rosé wine made in California.
- **Sparkling wine** Made by adding a yeast and sugar mixture to dry white or rosé wine and allowing a second fermentation to occur. Also made by introducing carbon dioxide gas to wine under pressure.
- **Organic wine** Made without artificial preservative from grapes that have been grown without the use of pesticides or artificial fertilizers.
- **Low alcohol wine** Ordinary wine from which the alcohol has been almost entirely removed by either a heat treatment process (which can drastically affect the flavour) or a cold filtration process.

Measuring alcoholic drink

Alcohol units

Alcohol is measured in units for the purposes of nutritional information and health advice. A unit is equivalent to 8 ml of alcohol. The table below gives unit equivalents for standard measures of alcoholic drinks. The unit values given are only approximate; different brands within these categories have a range of alcohol contents.

Alcoholic units per standard measure

Drink	Glass/measure	Units of alcohol
Beer • lager • cider	1 pt	2
Spirits • vodka, rum, whisky, gin, etc.	single measure 25 ml/1/6 gill	1
Wine	standard glass 114 ml/4 fl oz	1
Fortified wine • sherry, madeira, port, etc.	small glass 50 ml/1/3 gill	1

Buying wine

Wine labels often give details of the quality and type of wine as well as its name and the country/region of origin. Below are wine terms along with quality classifications, in ascending order, used by major wine producing nations (the higher the number, the better the quality of wine).

Austrian wine quality classifications and terms

Quality classifications

1 Tafelwein
2 Landwein
Qualitätsweins:
3 Kabinett
4 Spätlese
5 Auslese
6 Beerenauslese
7 Trockenbeerenauslese

Wine terms

Halbsüss	Medium sweet
Halbtrocken	Medium dry
Süss	Sweet
Trocken	Dry

Bulgarian wine quality classifications

Quality classifications

1 Country wines
2 Reserve
3 Controliran

French wine quality classifications and terms

Quality classifications

1 Vin de Table
2 Vin de Pays
3 VDQS (Vin Délimité de Qualité Supérieure)
4 Appellation Contrôlée:
The more specific the area identified the higher the standard of the wine, e.g. Appellation Bordeaux Contrôlée is of a lower standard than Appellation St Julien Contrôlée; St Julien being a specific area within the Bordeaux region.

Wine terms

Blanc de blancs	White wine made from white grapes only
Blanc de noirs	White wine made from black grapes only
Brut	A very dry sparkling wine
Claret	The English term for red wines from Bordeaux
Demi-sec	Medium dry
Doux	Sweet
Mis en bouteille au château	Bottled at the property where the grapes are grown
Nouveau/ Primeur	A very young wine from the latest harvest
Sec	Dry
Supérieur	High in alcohol content

German wine quality classifications and terms

Quality classifications

1 DTW (Deutscher Tafelwein)
2 Landwein
3 QbA (Qualitätswein eines Bestimmten Anbaugebietes)

QmP (Qualitätswein mit Prädikat):
4 Kabinett
5 Spätlese
6 Auslese
7 Beerenauslese
8 Trockenbeerenauslese

Wine terms

Deutscher sekt	Sparkling wine made from German grapes
Halbtrocken	Semi-dry
Rotwein	Red wine
Sekt	Sparkling wine made in Germany from non-German grapes
Trocken	Dry
Weissherbst	Rosé
Weisswein	White wine

Italian wine quality classifications and terms

Quality classifications

1 Vino da tavola
2 Vini Tipici (Indicazione Geografica Tipica)
3 DOC (Denominazione di Origine Controllata)
4 DOCG (Denominazione di Origine Controllata e Garantita

Wine terms

Abboccato	Medium to medium sweet
Amabile	Medium sweet
Asciutto	Dry
Bianco	White
Classico	From the best part of a wine growing area
Dolce	Sweet
Frizzante	Slightly sparkling
Riserva	Good wine which has been well aged
Rosato	Rosé
Rosso	Red
Secco	Dry
Spumante	Sparkling
Superiore	High in alcohol content

North American wine terms

Wine terms

Blush	An alternative name for rosé wines – often those made from a blend of grapes
White	Often applied to rosé wines

Portuguese wine quality classifications and terms

Quality classifications

1 Denominação de Origem
A paper seal bearing the words *sello de garantia* is fixed over the cork of all wines which have met this national standard.
2 Vinho de Mesa
3 Reserva
4 Garrafeira

Wine terms

Adamado	Sweet
Branco	White
Clarete	Rosé
Espumante	Sparkling
Sêco	Dry
Tinto	Red

Spanish wine quality classifications and terms

Quality classifications

1 Vino de Mesa
2 Vinos de la Tierra
3 DO (Denominación de Origen)
4 DOC (Denominación de Origen Calificada)

Wine terms

Blanco	White
Dulce	Sweet
Espumoso	Sparkling
Joven	A young wine
Rosado	Rosé
Seco	Dry
Tinto	Red

Storing and serving wine

Storing wine long term

- Store bottles on their sides in a purpose-made wine rack; this keeps the cork moist, preventing air from seeping into the bottle.
- Store wine away from draughts in a place with a cool, consistent temperature.
- Keep bottles away from direct or strong light.

Storing wine short term

Once wine is exposed to air it quickly begins to deteriorate with the action of microorganisms. To avoid wine going off:

- Reseal opened bottles and keep them in the fridge. Wine should remain palatable in this state for about 24 hours.
- Wine boxes use one-way valves to dispense wine without letting in air and keep the wine in good condition for up to 2 weeks.
- Reseal opened bottles with a device which allows you to pump the air out of the bottle. This allows wine to be kept for up to a week.

Decanting wine

Vintage red wines and ports naturally generate a sediment while in the bottle. Decanting is the process of separating this sediment (which is perfectly harmless) from the wine. Decanting also helps to fully aerate wine and can improve the flavour of virtually any red wine. To decant a wine:

1. Stand the bottle upright for two days before you begin. This allows time for the sediment to settle at the bottom.
2. Clean the wine decanter thoroughly with hot water. Do not use detergent; it may leave a residue which will affect the flavour of the wine.
3. Open the bottle very carefully; if it is an old wine the cork may be brittle.
4. Place the decanter at eye level in front of a light source. Place a clean funnel in the neck of the decanter.

5 Pour the wine very slowly, and without stopping, into the funnel. The light will allow you to see the sediment in the bottle and avoid letting any into the decanter.

6 As soon as you see sediment enter the neck of the bottle, stop pouring. The little wine left in the bottle can be poured straight into a glass and left to settle for tasting or for use in cooking.

Allowing wine to breathe

All red and rosé wines (apart from new Beaujolais or other very young wines) should be allowed to breathe before they are served. 'Breathing' (also called 'aerating') means allowing air to interact with the wine. This is done by simply opening the bottle and leaving it to stand at room temperature for one to two hours.

Wine serving temperatures

To get the best from wine it needs to be served at the correct temperature. The exact temperature depends on personal taste and the particular wine in question, but there are a few guidelines which should generally produce good results:

- Red wines should be left to stand at room temperature for one to two hours.
- Never attempt to warm red wine quickly by heating it directly; this will certainly damage the flavour.
- White wines should be chilled in the fridge for an hour to an hour and a half.
- If time is short, white wines can be chilled quickly in the freezer, although this fierce cooling produces less than perfect results.

Recommended serving temperatures for wine

Type of wine	Temperature
Mature, full flavoured reds	18 °C (65 °F)
Medium reds	16 °C (60 °F)
Rosés and young Beaujolais	12 °C (54 °F)
Dry whites	10 °C (50 °F)
Sparkling whites and champagne	7 °C (45 °F)
Sweet whites (dessert wines)	6 °C (42 °F)

Which wine to serve

The choice of wine to accompany a meal is entirely down to personal taste. The only way to discover which wine goes well with which meal is to experiment. There are a few guidelines which generally produce good results:

- With red meats drink dry red wine.
- With most white meats (including fish) drink white wine.
- Try to match the wine to the dominant flavour of the dish rather than just the colour of the meat. For example, a fish dish served with a strong tomato and herb sauce will probably be better accompanied by a full flavoured red wine than a delicate white.
- Certain foods do not go well with wine. Strong curries and other very spicy dishes, vinegar dressings and rich chocolate tend to overpower the taste of any wine.

Serving order for wine

With a large, formal meal a different wine may be drunk with each course. For best results serve wines in this order:

- Dry wines should be served before sweet wines.
- White wines should be served before red wines.
- Delicate wines should be served before full-bodied wines.
- The best wine should be served last.

Cooking with alcoholic drink

Tips for cooking with alcoholic drink

- It is the flavour of wine rather than its alcohol content which improves foods during cooking; do not use poor quality wines for cooking any more than you would for drinking.
- Fish, veal and chicken are complemented by medium-dry white wines.
- Lamb, beef and game are complemented by dry red wines. The stronger the flavour of the dish the fuller the red wine that should be used.
- An all-purpose marinade can by made by adding a bouquet garni (herbs), chopped garlic and onion to one part olive oil and three parts dry red or white wine (depending on the meat to be marinated).
- When using spirits to flame a dish pour the spirit into a metal ladle first and warm it gently over a naked flame; it will burn much more easily when poured over the dish.
- Marinate fresh fruits in a fruit liqueur to enhance their flavour for sweet puddings or fruit salads.

TEA AND COFFEE

Types of tea

The three main types of tea differ in the method used to process the leaves.

Black tea

This is made from leaves which have been fermented before drying and packing. It produces a dark, strong-tasting brew. Examples are:

- **Assam** Grown in the Indian province of Assam. Produces a brew with a distinctive red tint.
- **Camomile** Tea which has been flavoured with dried camomile flowers. Reputed to be a relaxant.
- **Ceylon** Originating in Sri Lanka (formerly called Ceylon), its exceptional flavour is preserved by a special drying process.
- **Darjeeling** Grown on the foot hills of the Himalayas near the Indian town of Darjeeling. One of India's finest teas.
- **Earl Grey** A blend of Indian and Sri Lankan teas made to a Chinese recipe discovered by Earl Grey in the early 19th century. Its distinctive flavour comes from bergamot oil.
- **English breakfast** A blend of several teas (usually Ceylon and Assam) which produces a full-flavoured brew.
- **Irish breakfast** A blend of teas similar to **English breakfast**.
- **Lapsang souchong** Grown in the Chinese province of Fukian. It has a distinctive smoky flavour.

Green tea

This is made from leaves which have been steamed and dried but not fermented. It produces a pale yellowish brew with a bitter taste.

- **Gunpowder** The finest Chinese green tea. Leaves are rolled into tiny balls giving the dry tea a granular appearance. It produces a pale brew with a sharp flavour.
- **Matcha** A very fine Japanese tea (used in traditional Japanese tea ceremonies). Leaves are crushed to make a bright green powder. It produces a brew with a very bitter taste.
- **Tencha** The finest Japanese green tea.

Oolong tea

This is made with leaves which have been partially fermented before drying and packing. It produces a brew with characteristics midway between black and green teas.

- **Formosa Oolong** Grown in Taiwan (formerly called Formosa) and considered to be one of the finest teas in the world. It produces a pale yellow brew with a fruity flavour.

Other kinds of tea

Blended tea Made from a variety of teas blended together. Most commercial tea brands are blends which are combined with great skill to produce a consistent and distinct flavour.

Herb tea Made with various combinations of herbs and spices and usually does not include tea leaves at all. Herb teas are also known as *Tisanes*.

Instant tea Made by brewing large quantities of tea (usually a blend) which is dehydrated to form granules. These granules produce instant tea when rehydrated with hot water.

Speciality tea There is a huge variety of tea blends flavoured with herbs, spices and other ingredients. Common flavourings include orange and jasmine.

Tea leaf sizes

All loose teas (i.e. those not sold in teabags) are categorized according to leaf size:

- **Orange pekoe** Small leaves
- **Pekoe** Medium leaves
- **Pekoe souchong** Large leaves

Types of coffee

There are hundreds of varieties of coffee plant but they are all derived from either the *Coffea arabica* or the *Coffea robusta*. *Coffea arabica* is generally considered to produce superior, subtle flavours. It is grown at high altitudes and is the dominant variety in South America. *Coffea robusta* produces more pungent flavours and can tolerate a greater range of climates. It is the dominant variety in Africa.

Coffee bean roasts

An important factor affecting coffee flavour is the length of time the beans are roasted before packing:

Dark roast Produces a very dark brown bean which makes strong, richly flavoured coffee. French, Italian and Turkish coffees are usually dark roasts.

Medium roast Produces a dark brown bean which

makes medium strength coffee with plenty of flavour.
Expresso roast A blend of two parts dark roast and one part medium roast.
Viennese roast A blend of two parts medium roast and one part dark roast.
Blended roast Almost all commercial brands of coffee are a blend of dark and medium roast beans from a range of coffee varieties. Breakfast coffee is a blended roast coffee.

Other types of coffee
Instant coffee Can be made from any blend of coffee. It is reduced to granules by evaporation or freeze drying and is easily rehydrated by adding hot water.
Decaffeinated coffee Caffeine is removed from coffee beans before roasting either by using a solvent or by scraping off the caffeine-rich skins of the bean after softening them with steam.

Coffee preparations
Café au lait Equal measures of coffee and scalded milk.
Café brûlot Coffee blended with spices, citrus peel and brandy. It is flamed before serving.
Café latte Expresso coffee mixed with lots of hot, foaming milk.
Café mocha Expresso coffee mixed with chocolate syrup and lots of foaming milk.
Cappuccino Expresso coffee topped with the foam from steamed milk.
Expresso A strong coffee made by forcing steam through finely ground coffee.

Greek/Turkish A very strong coffee made by repeatedly boiling finely ground coffee and selected spices in water.
Irish Strong coffee mixed with Irish whiskey and topped with a dollop of whipped cream.
Thai Coffee mixed with sweetened condensed milk.
Viennese Strong coffee, sweetened and topped with a dollop of whipped cream.

Storage times for tea and coffee

Type	Duration
Tea	
• sealed	12–18 months
• opened	2–3 weeks
Coffee, beans	
• sealed	9 months
• opened	1 week
Coffee, ground	
• sealed	18 months
• opened	1 week
Coffee, instant	
• sealed	12–18 months
• opened	4 weeks

5. Health and nutrition

Food contains proteins, carbohydrates, fats, vitamins and minerals. Each of these nutrients is used by the body in different ways. Good health depends on properly balancing your intake of them; eating neither too much nor too little of any one. This section begins by describing both the benefits and hazards of various food substances, including food additives. There are also calorie tables, advice on reading food labels and tips on achieving a healthy balanced diet.

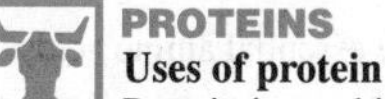

PROTEINS

Uses of protein

Protein is used in the body to help build and repair cells. It can also be converted into carbohydrate to provide energy.

Types of protein

Proteins are complex substances made from chemicals called amino acids. The body can manufacture most of the amino acids that it needs, but there are eight that can only be derived from food. They are called essential amino acids. Most animal products contain all the essential amino acids required by the body and are therefore sometimes referred to as complete proteins.

Health considerations

- Most vegetables contain very little protein and a diet of only vegetables rarely supplies the daily requirement of essential amino acids. Vegetarians

who also eat eggs, cheese and other dairy products are rarely at risk, but vegans should supplement their diet with alternative protein-rich foods.
- Protein-rich alternatives to meat that contain all the essential amino acids are also suitable for people wanting to eat protein-rich foods which do not contain animal products.

Sources of protein

Protein can be obtained from both animal and plant sources.
- Foods rich in essential amino acids include meat, fish and dairy products.
- Foods containing some of the essential amino acids include beans, grains and nuts.
- Protein-rich foods suitable for vegetarians include texturized vegetable protein developed from soya beans and mycoprotein produced from fungal microorganisms; also tofu (bean curd) and miso (fermented bean paste) in Far Eastern cuisine.

Sources of protein

CARBOHYDRATES

Uses of carbohydrates

Carbohydrates provide the body with energy. They may also be converted into body fat for storage.

Types of carbohydrate

There are three major groups of carbohydrates:

- **Sugars** These provide the body with energy in a form that can be used very quickly. The main types of sugars are glucose, fructose, lactose, sucrose and maltose.
- **Starches** These provide the body with energy over a longer period of time.
- **Fibre** These are substances found in the cell walls of plants, and form an important part of the human diet. Only some fibre is digestible.

Health considerations

- Eating a lot of foods with high sugar content, especially between meals, is associated with increased tooth decay. High sugar intake is also likely to lead to weight increase/fat.
- Digestible fibre can reduce the amount of cholesterol in the blood and help lower the risk of heart disease.
- Non-digestible fibre can help to prevent digestive disorders.

Sources of carbohydrate

The body cannot manufacture carbohydrates and so must obtain them from food.

- Foods rich in *sugars* include soft drinks, honey, cakes, biscuits, chocolate, ice-cream and other

processed or pre-packaged foods with sugar added.
- Foods rich in *starches* include bread, potatoes, cakes, biscuits and other cereal products.
- Foods rich in *fibre* include raw fruit, wholemeal bread and pasta, wholewheat cereals, oatmeal, peas, beans, lentils, potatoes in their skins, dried fruits and nuts.

Sources of carbohydrates

FATS

Uses of fats

Fats are the body's most concentrated source of energy. Fat stored in the body in fat cells can be converted to energy when needed and provides insulation and padding to protect the body from injury.

Types of fats

There are two main types of fat in foods:
- **Saturated fats (saturates)** These are mostly animal fats, although vegetable fats can also be mainly saturates. They contain a high proportion of hydrogen atoms in their chemical make-up and are

usually solid at room temperature. Saturates are believed to be harmful to health; they are non-essential and can be replaced by other energy sources.

- **Unsaturated fats (unsaturates)** These are mainly vegetable fats and are liquid (in the form of an oil) at room temperature. There are two kinds of unsaturates:
  - *Monounsaturated fats*, which have fewer hydrogen atoms in their structure than saturated fats.
  - *Polyunsaturated fats*, which have the fewest hydrogen atoms in their structure.

  Both monounsaturated and polyunsaturated fats are considered to be less harmful to health than saturated fats, and some are essential to health.

Health considerations

- A high intake of saturated fat can lead to an increased level of cholesterol in the blood. Deposits of cholesterol on the walls of blood vessels can eventually lead to narrowing and blockage of arteries that supply the heart with blood. Current recommendations are that we should eat less saturated fat.
- Monounsaturates and polyunsaturates in the diet can reduce the levels of cholesterol in the blood and may help to prevent heart disease. Current recommendations are that we should use unsaturated fats in preference to saturated fats.
- Certain polyunsaturates, known as Omega-3 oils, may help to prevent heart disease and may also benefit brain growth and development. Current

recommendations are that we should eat more Omega-3 polyunsaturates.
- Some unsaturated oils are artificially solidified in a process known as hydrogenation. This process creates *trans fatty acids*, converting the oil mixture into a saturated fat and removing any benefits it had as an unsaturate. Current recommendations are that the amount of trans fatty acids in people's diets should be decreased.

Sources of fats

- Foods high in saturates include butter, lard, suet, hydrogenated (hard) vegetable margarine, coconut oil, cheese, pastry, meat and full-fat milk.
- Foods high in monounsaturates include olive oil, peanut oil, biscuits and peanuts.
- Foods high in polyunsaturates include vegetable seed oils, e.g. corn (maize) oil, sunflower oil and sesame oil.
- Sources of Omega-3 polyunsaturates include oily fish, e.g. sardines, herring and mackerel.

Sources of fats

Fat composition

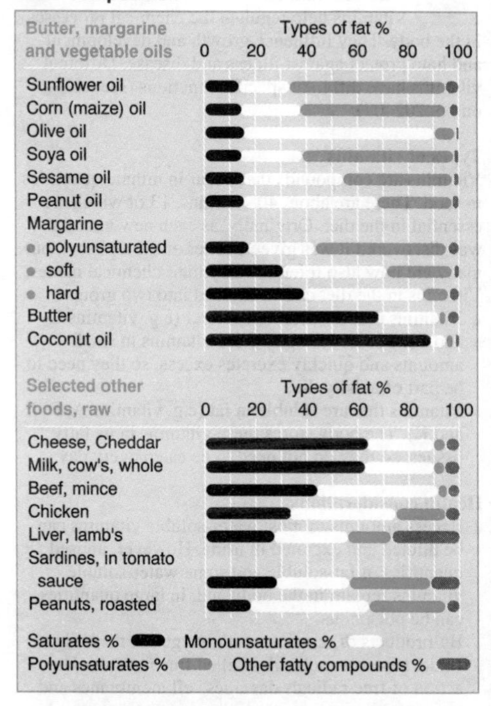

VITAMINS

Uses of vitamins

Vitamins help regulate the chemical processes in the body. They influence growth and development and help protect against illness and disease. Different vitamins have different specific functions (see tables on pp. 202–07).

Types of vitamins

Vitamins are compounds that occur in minute quantities in food. There are about 40 vitamins, 13 of which are essential in the diet. Originally, as each new vitamin was discovered it was given a letter of the alphabet, but many are now also referred to by their chemical names. Vitamins in the diet can be divided into two groups:

- Vitamins that are soluble in water (e.g. vitamins C and B). The body stores these vitamins in small amounts and quickly excretes excess, so they need to be part of a daily diet.
- Vitamins that are soluble in fat (e.g. vitamins A, D, E and K). The body stores these vitamins in its fatty tissues, so they do not need to be eaten every day.

Health considerations

- Excess amounts of most water-soluble vitamins can be diluted and excreted in urine. However, unused quantities of fat-soluble and some water-soluble vitamins remain in the body and, in large quantities, can be poisonous.
- By-products of reactions with oxygen in the body create unstable molecules called free radicals. The action of free radicals damages cell membranes and

can promote the formation of cancer cells. Antioxidants such as vitamin E appear to block the action of free radicals before cell damage can take place.

Sources of vitamins

The body can manufacture vitamin D (from sunlight), and pyridoxine, a B vitamin (from bacteria in the intestine). All other vitamins must come from food.

- Water-soluble vitamins are found in a variety of plant and animal foods.
- Fat-soluble vitamins are found mainly in foods containing oil and fat.

For a detailed list of sources see the tables on pp. 202–07.

Sources of vitamins

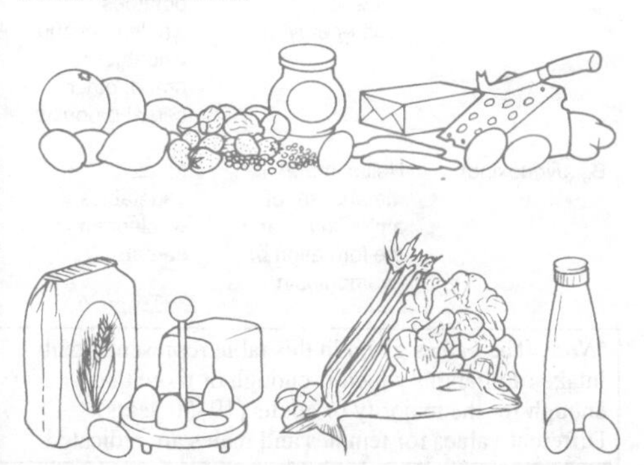

Water-soluble vitamins

Name	Function	Food sources
B_1 (thiamin)	Helps in the steady release of energy from carbohydrate	Milk, offal, pork, fruit, potatoes, wholegrain cereals, eggs
B_2 (riboflavin)	Helps in carbohydrate and protein metabolism	Milk, eggs, liver, kidney, cereal products
Niacin	Helps in the utlization of food energy	Liver, chicken, potatoes, wholemeal and wheatgerm bread, other cereal products
B_6 (pyridoxine)	Helps in the metabolism of amino acids and the formation of haemoglobin	Meat, vegetables, wholegrain cereals

**Note:* The values given in this table represent a daily intake of vitamins which is enough or more than enough for the majority of adults (19–50 years). Different values for females and males are indicated

1 g = 1000 mg
1 g = 1 000 000 μg

Deficiency results in	Excess results in	Daily nutrient requirements*
Beriberi (pain, paralysis and swelling to limbs)	Excreted	F: 0.8 mg M: 1.0 mg
Blurred vision, bloodshot eyes, sores in corners of the mouth	Mainly excreted; some stored in liver, kidney and heart	F: 1.1 mg M: 1.3 mg
Pellagra (dermatitis, diarrhoea, nervous and mental disorders)	Flushing and liver damage in some people	F: 13 mg M: 17 mg
Lesions to lips and mouth, fatigue, anaemia; deficiency is rare	Very high intakes (more than 50 mg per day) can affect sensory nerve function	F: 1.2 mg M: 1.4 mg

continued

by the letters 'F' and 'M'. Recommended intakes for children, pregnant women and the elderly are given in the Department of Health's publication *Dietary Reference Values*, 1991.

Water-soluble vitamins (continued)

Name	Function	Food sources
Pantothenic acid	Helps release energy from fat and carbohydrate	Cereals, beans, peas, animal products
Folate (folic acid)	Helps form red blood cells and genetic material	Liver, raw leaf salads, eggs, cereals, peas, beans
B_{12} (cyanocobalamin)	Helps form red blood cells and operate nervous system	Liver, muscle meats, fish, dairy products (not present in plant foods)
Biotin	Helps breakdown fatty acids and release energy from carbohydrates and amino acids	Liver, egg yolk, cereals, fish, fruit, milk, soya flour, vegetables
C (ascorbic acid)	Helps maintain bones, and connective tissue; acts as an antioxidant (*see* pp. 200–01)	Many fruits and vegetables, especially citrus fruits and blackcurrants

**See* note on p. 202 for an explanation of these figures

Deficiency results in	Excess results in	Daily nutrient requirements*
Deficiency symptoms very rare	Excreted	No set requirement
Megaloblastic anaemia (abnormal red blood cell production)	No known ill effects	200 µg
Pernicious anaemia and degeneration of nerve cells	Excreted; some is conserved	1.5 µg
Anaemia, loss of appetite, fatigue, nausea, muscle pains, dry skin, high blood cholesterol	No ill effects reported in up to 10 mg per day intake	No set requirement
Poor healing of wounds; bleeding under the skin and from gums; scurvy	Excreted; excessive intakes can lead to diarrhoea	40 mg

Fat-soluble vitamins

Name	Function	Food sources
A (retinol)	Needed for maintenance of skin, lining tissues, bones, teeth and hair, and for dim-light vision	Liver, kidney, eggs, milk, butter, cheese, green vegetables, carrots, margarine
D (calciferol)	Required for absorption of calcium; needed for growth and maintenance of bones and teeth	Cod-liver oil, oily fish, margarine, eggs, dairy products, liver
E (tocopherol)	Helps form red blood cells; acts as an antioxidant (helps protect cells from damage)	Vegetable oil, nuts, whole grain cereals and cereal products, egg yolk, milk
K	Essential for normal clotting of blood	Green leafy vegetables, peas, cereals, eggs, liver

*See note on p. 202 for an explanation of these figures

Deficiency results in	Excess results in	Daily nutrient requirements*
Night blindness, dry eyes, eye fatigue	Large amounts accumulate in the liver and can be poisonous. High amounts of retinol in pregnant women can cause birth defects	F: 600 µg M: 700 µg
Rickets (bone deformities) in children; osteomalacia (bone softening) in adults	Causes too much calcium to be absorbed; the excess can damage the kidneys	No dietary intake usually needed (main source is sunlight on skin)
Anaemia; fluid retention	Very high intakes do not appear to be toxic	No set requirement
Haemorrhaging; deficiency very rare	Liver damage in the newborn	No set requirement

MINERALS

Uses of minerals

Minerals have three main functions:

- As soluble salts which help to control the composition of body fluids and cells.
- As constituents of bones and teeth.
- As essential elements in the release and utilization of energy.

The tables on pp. 210–17 give information on the particular functions of different minerals.

Types of minerals

More than 20 minerals are needed by the body.

- Major minerals are needed in relatively large amounts.
- Trace minerals (elements) are needed in smaller quantities but are no less important for the body's functioning than the major minerals.

Health considerations

- Most trace minerals can be poisonous in excess.
- Sodium is a mineral found in salt (sodium chloride). Too much sodium can cause high blood pressure so many people now take care to limit their salt intake. The table opposite gives quantities of sodium found in various foods.

Sources of minerals

The tables on pp. 210–17 provide information on the sources of particular minerals.

Sources of minerals

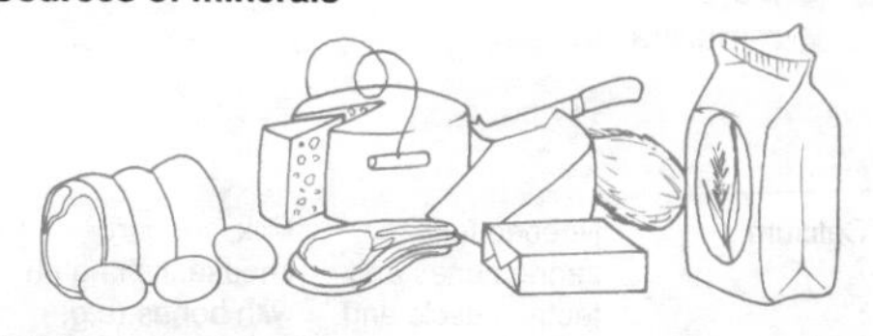

Sodium (salt) content of selected foods

Food type	Sodium content (mg per 100 g)
Bananas	1
Orange juice	2
Peas, frozen	3
Butter, unsalted	11
Haddock, fresh	120
Peas, canned, processed	380
Bread, wholemeal	550
Butter, salted	750
Margarine	800
Potato crisps	1070
Haddock, smoked	1220
Bacon, streaky	1500
Soy sauce	5720
Gravy instant granules	6330

Note: The sodium content of vegetables is much higher if they are cooked in salted water.

Major minerals

Name	Function	Food sources
Calcium	Needed for strong bones and teeth, muscle and nerve functioning, and blood clotting	Milk, yoghurt, cheese, fish eaten with bones (e.g. sardines), peas, beans and other vegetables
Chloride	Regulates fluid balance in the body; forms part of gastric juice	Salt or any products with added salt
Magnesium	Needed for bone and teeth formation and energy utilization	Green leafy vegetables, wholegrain foods, nuts, seeds, peas, beans, milk

Note: The values given in this table represent a daily intake of minerals which is enough or more than enough for the majority of adults (19–50 years). Different values for females and males are indicated

1 g = 1000 mg
1 g = 1 000 000 μg

Deficiency results in	Excess results in	Daily nutrient requirements*
Stunted growth and rickets (leg bone deformities) in children; osteomalacia (decalcified bones) in adults	Vomiting, diarrhoea, kidney damage	700 mg
Muscle cramps, loss of appetite, mental apathy	Vomiting, dehydration	2500 mg
Muscular tremors, anxiety, depression	Diarrhoea, nausea, vomiting, lethargy and muscle weakness	F: 270 mg M: 300 mg

continued

by the letters 'F' and 'M'. Recommended intakes for children, pregnant women and the elderly are given in the Department of Health's publication *Dietary Reference Values*, 1991.

Major minerals (continued)

Name	Function	Food sources
Phosphorus	Needed to maintain strong and healthy bones and teeth; involved in release of energy	Milk, cheese, white meat, fish, whole grains, nuts, peas, beans
Potassium	Helps to regulate fluid content of cells	Many fruit and vegetables, especially potatoes and bananas; salt, cereals and meat
Sodium	Helps maintain fluid balance	Salt, yeast extract, bacon, kippers, many processed foods
Sulphur	Constituent of cartilage, hair and nails	Meat, fish, eggs, peas, beans

*See note on p. 210 for an explanation of these figures

Deficiency results in	Excess results in	Daily nutrient requirements*
Deficiency unknown – phosphorus is in most foods	High intakes in first few days of birth may produce muscle spasms	550 mg
Muscular weakness, abnormal heart rhythm; deficiency rare – potassium is in many foods	Kidney damage, heart failure in severe cases	3500 mg
Muscular cramps, loss of appetite, apathy, fainting	High blood pressure, kidney damage in children	1600 mg
Not known	Not known	No set requirement

Trace minerals

Name	Function	Food sources
Chromium	Helps insulin work in the utilization of glucose	Brewers' yeast, meat, wholegrain cereals, peas, beans, nuts
Copper	Component of many enzymes; needed for iron absorption and metabolism	Liver, shellfish, meat, bread and other cereal products, peas, beans, nuts
Fluoride	Needed for maintenance of teeth and bones	Fluoridated drinking water, tea, seafood
Iodine	Needed to form thyroid hormones for utilization of nutrients	Seafood, cereals, iodized salt, milk, vegetables
Iron	Constituent of haemoglobin in blood; needed to transport oxygen from lungs to cells	Liver, kidney and other meat; vegetables, egg yolk, whole grain bread

*See note on p. 210 for an explanation of these figures

Deficiency results in	Excess results in	Daily nutrient requirements*
Raised blood sugar	Skin and kidney damage	No set requirement
Stunted growth, anaemia in children, heart function defects	Nausea, vomiting, diarrhoea, cirrhosis, brain damage	1.2 mg
Dental decay	Discolouration of teeth	No set requirement
Enlarged thyroid gland; mental development in young inhibited	Inhibits thyroid function	140 µg
Tiredness, anaemia	Cirrhosis of the liver	F: 14.8 mg M: 8.7 mg

continued

1 g = 1000 mg
1 g = 1 000 000 µg

Trace minerals (continued)

Name	Function	Food sources
Manganese	Component of certain enzymes; activates other enzymes	Tea, green leafy vegetables, peas, beans, nuts, spices, whole grain cereals
Molybdenum	Essential in metabolism	Peas, beans, whole grain bread and cereal products, milk
Selenium	Helps protect cells from oxidative damage	Liver, kidney, seafood, whole grain bread and cereal products
Zinc	Helps with the healing of wounds, tissue repair, growth; associated with activity of many enzymes	Red meat and meat products, seafood, whole grain bread and other cereal products, milk, eggs

**See* note on p. 210 for an explanation of these figures

Deficiency results in	Excess results in	Daily nutrient requirements*
Not known	Nervous and mental disorders; reported reactions rare	No set requirement
Not known	May cause altered metabolism	No set requirement
Damage to intracellular structures	Vomiting	F: 60 µg M: 75 µg
Loss of appetitie, hair loss, diarrhoea, slow healing of wounds; in children, impairs growth and delays sexual development	Fever, vomiting, diarrhoea	F: 7 mg M: 9.5 mg

FOOD AND ENERGY

Calories and joules

Food provides our bodies with energy. The metric (SI) unit of energy is the joule. In nutrition, the energy derived from food is measured in kilojoules (kJ).

1 kilojoule (kJ) = 1000 joules

Although the kilojoule has officially replaced the kilocalorie, many people still talk in terms of calories. A calorie is defined as the amount of energy needed to raise the temperature of 1 cubic centimetre of water by 1 °Centigrade. The energy derived from food is usually referred to in terms of kilocalories (kcal).

1 kilocalorie (kcal) = 1000 calories

Some food labels use the term 'Calorie' (i.e. with a capital 'C') or simply 'calorie' to refer to a kilocalorie.

The factor used for conversion between kilocalories and kilojoules is:

1 kilocalorie (kcal) = 4.19 kilojoules (kJ)

Conversion

kcal ⟶ kJ x 4.19

Energy in different foods

Different nutrients provide us with different amounts of energy. For example, a gram of carbohydrate provides 17 kJ but a gram of fat provides 38 kJ. Replacing fats with carbohydrates in the diet is a good way to reduce calorie intake.

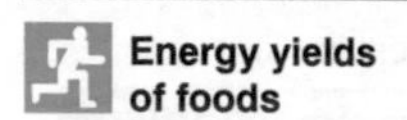

Energy yields of foods

Food	Energy yield kJ per g/ml	Energy yield kcal per g/ml
Fats	38	9
Carbohydrates	17	4
Proteins	17	4
Vitamins	0	0
Minerals	0	0
Water	0	0
Fibre	0	0

Food and drink calorie table

(energy per 100 g/100 ml of edible portion)

Food/drink	Energy per 100 g/100 ml	
Alcoholic drinks	**kJ**	**kcal**
Beer, bitter	130	31
Cider, dry	151	36
Lager, bottled	122	29
Spirits, 40% volume	930	222
Wine, white, medium	314	75
Wine, red	285	68
Beverages	**kJ**	**kcal**
Cocoa powder	1307	312
Coffee, infusion 5 minutes	8	2

continued

Food and drink calorie table (continued)

Food/drink	Energy per 100 g/100 ml	
Beverages (continued)	**kJ**	**kcal**
Coffee, instant powder	419	100
Drinking chocolate powder	1534	366
Tea, without milk	0	0
Breads	**kJ**	**kcal**
Brown bread	913	218
White bread	985	235
White bread with added fibre	964	230
Wholemeal bread	901	215
Cereals	**kJ**	**kcal**
Corn flakes	1508	360
Flour, plain, white	1428	341
Flour, wholemeal	1299	310
Muesli	1521	363
Oats, porridge, raw	1571	375
Rice, brown, boiled	591	141
Rice, white, boiled	578	138
Spaghetti, white, boiled	436	104
Cheese	**kJ**	**kcal**
Brie	1336	319
Cheddar	1726	412

continued

Food and drink calorie table (continued)

Food/drink	Energy per 100 g/100 ml	
Cheese (continued)	kJ	kcal
Cheese spread	1156	276
Cottage cheese	411	98
Fromage frais, fruit added	549	131
Eggs	kJ	kcal
Eggs, hens', boiled	616	147
Eggs, hens', fried	750	179
Fats and oils	kJ	kcal
Butter	3088	737
Low-fat spread	1634	390
Margarine, polyunsaturated	3096	739
Sunflower seed oil	3767	899
Fish and fish products	kJ	kcal
Cod in batter, fried in vegetable oil	834	199
Fish fingers, grilled	897	214
Haddock, steamed	411	98
Herring, grilled	834	199
Mackerel, fried	788	188
Pilchards, canned in tomato sauce	528	126
Prawns, boiled	448	107
Sardines, canned in oil, drained	909	217

continued

Food and drink calorie table (continued)

Food/drink	Energy per 100 g/100 ml	
Fish and fish products (continued)	**kJ**	**kcal**
Tuna, canned in brine, drained	448	107
Fruit	**kJ**	**kcal**
Apples, eating, raw	197	47
Apricots, raw	117	28
Apricots, stewed with sugar	251	60
Avocado	796	190
Bananas	398	95
Blackcurrants, stewed with sugar	247	59
Cherries, raw, weighed without stones	201	48
Dates, dried, weighed without stones	1131	270
Figs, dried	876	209
Gooseberries, stewed with sugar	210	50
Grapefruit, raw	126	30
Grapes	252	60
Kiwi fruit	205	49
Mangoes, ripe	239	57
Melon, honeydew	117	28
Oranges	155	37
Peaches, canned in syrup	272	65
Peaches, raw	138	33
Pears, raw	168	40
Pineapple, canned in juice	222	53
Plums, raw	151	36
Prunes	591	141

continued

Food and drink calorie table (continued)

Food/drink	Energy per 100 g/100 ml	
Fruit (continued)	kJ	kcal
Raspberries, raw	105	25
Rhubarb, stewed with sugar	189	45
Strawberries, raw	113	27
Sultanas	1048	250
Meat	kJ	kcal
Bacon, back rasher, fried	1948	465
Bacon, back rasher, grilled	1697	405
Beef, lean, roast	821	196
Beef, mince, stewed	960	229
Beefburgers, frozen, fried	1106	264
Chicken, boiled, no skin	767	183
Chicken, roast, meat and skin	905	216
Chicken, roast, no skin	620	148
Corned beef, canned	909	217
Kidney, pig, stewed	641	153
Lamb, chops, grilled	930	222
Lamb, roast, no skin	1115	266
Liver, chicken, fried	813	194
Liver, lamb, fried	972	232
Paté, liver	1324	316
Pork chops, loin, lean only, grilled	947	226
Pork, roast, lean and fat	1198	286
Salami	2057	491
Sausages, beef, grilled	1110	265

continued

Food and drink calorie table (continued)

Food/drink	Energy per 100 g/100 ml	
Meat (continued)	**kJ**	**kcal**
Sausage, low fat, grilled	960	229
Sausages, pork, grilled	1332	318
Steak and kidney pie, individual	1353	323
Turkey, roast, meat and skin	716	171
Milk and milk products	**kJ**	**kcal**
Cream, fresh, single	830	198
Dried skimmed milk	210	50
Evaporated milk	270	64
Semi-skimmed milk	193	46
Skimmed milk	138	33
Whole milk	277	66
Yoghurt, low fat	197	47
Yoghurt, whole milk, fruit	440	105
Yoghurt, whole milk, plain	331	79
Nuts	**kJ**	**kcal**
Almonds	2564	612
Coconut, dessicated	2531	604
Peanut butter (smooth)	2610	623
Peanuts, roasted and salted	2522	602

continued

Food and drink calorie table (continued)

Food/drink	Energy per 100 g/100 ml	
Potatoes and potato products	**kJ**	**kcal**
Chips, fried in vegetable oil	792	189
Oven chips, frozen, baked	679	162
Potato crisps	2288	546
Potatoes, new, boiled	318	76
Potatoes, old, baked, flesh and skin	356	85
Potatoes, old, boiled	335	80
Potatoes, old, mashed	499	119
Potatoes, old, roasted in vegetable oil	624	149
Soft drinks and juices	**kJ**	**kcal**
Cola	163	39
Lemonade, bottled	88	21
Orange drink, undiluted	448	107
Orange juice, unsweetened	151	36
Pineapple juice, unsweetened	172	41
Sugars and preserves	**kJ**	**kcal**
Honey	1207	288
Jam, fruit	1094	261
Maple syrup	1048	250
Marmalade	1094	261
Peppermints	1642	392
Sugar, white	1651	394
Syrup, golden	1249	298

continued

Food and drink calorie table (continued)

Food/drink	Energy per 100 g/100 ml	
Sweet foods	**kJ**	**kcal**
Bread pudding	1244	297
Cheesecake, frozen	1014	242
Chocolate biscuits	2196	524
Chocolate, milk	2221	530
Currant buns	1240	296
Custard made with whole milk	490	117
Digestive biscuits, plain	1973	471
Fruit cake, rich	1429	341
Fruit pie	1089	260
Jam tarts	1542	368
Rice pudding, canned	373	89
Swiss roll, individual	1412	337
Trifle	670	160
Vegetables	**kJ**	**kcal**
Aubergine, raw	63	15
Beans, baked, canned, tomato sauce	352	84
Beans, red kidney, canned, drained	419	100
Beans, runner, boiled	75	18
Beetroot, boiled	193	46
Brussels sprouts	147	35
Cabbage, boiled	38	19
Cabbage, raw	109	26
Carrots, old, boiled	101	24
Cauliflower, boiled	117	28

continued

Food and drink calorie table (continued)

Food/drink	Energy per 100 g/100 ml	
Vegetables (continued)	**kJ**	**kcal**
Celery, raw	29	7
Courgette, raw	75	18
Cucumber	42	10
Lentils, (red) boiled	419	100
Lettuce	59	14
Mushrooms, raw	54	13
Onions, raw	151	36
Parsnips, boiled	277	66
Peas frozen, boiled	289	69
Peppers, green, raw	63	15
Plantain, boiled	469	112
Processed peas, canned, re-heated	415	99
Spinach, frozen, boiled	88	21
Sweetcorn, canned, reheated	511	122
Sweet potato, boiled	352	84
Tofu (soya bean curd), steamed	306	73
Tomatoes, raw	71	17
Turnip, boiled	50	12
Watercress	92	22
Yam, boiled	557	133
Miscellaneous	**kJ**	**kcal**
Mayonnaise	2895	691
Mustard	582	139
Mycoprotein	360	86

continued

Food and drink calorie table (continued)

Food/drink **Miscellaneous** (continued)	Energy per 100 g/100 ml **kJ**	 **kcal**
Pickle, sweet	561	134
Salad cream	1458	348
Soup, cream of tomato, canned	230	55
Soy sauce	268	64
Tomato ketchup	411	98

Note: Calorific values for cooked foods are for 100 g of food weighed after cooking.

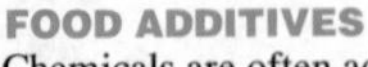

FOOD ADDITIVES

Chemicals are often added to foods as preservatives, to add colour, to help different food substances combine in processed foods (e.g. cakes and biscuits), and to enhance the taste and texture of food. These chemicals are known as additives. Most additives included in a product must be listed on the packaging label.

E numbers

Additives which have been approved usually have numbers. Those with an E number (a number with the prefix E) have been approved by the European Union (EU). A number without an E prefix refers to an additive which has been approved by the UK but not by the EU. Some additives approved in the UK will not be given a number until the EU gives them one; they are identified by name on food labels.

Natural or man-made?
An additive with an E number is simply an additive that has been approved by the European Union; it does not mean that the additive is man-made rather than natural. Additives listed in the table on pp. 230–245 include the following types:

- Natural additives, e.g. red colouring derived from beetroot juice (E162).
- Man-made compounds which are also found in nature, e.g. potassium nitrate (E252).
- Man-made compounds which are not found in nature, e.g. saccharin – a low calorie sweetener.

Safety
Both natural and man-made additives go through the same safety screening. Any additive that has been approved in the UK and by the EU is considered safe for almost everyone, although it is possible a few people may react badly to it. Approved additives do not come with an absolute guarantee of safety.

Types of additives
Antioxidants These additives stop fatty foods from going rancid. They also prevent fat-soluble vitamins (*see* pp. 206–07) being lost through oxidation.

Colours Sometimes the processing of food destroys its colour. Colorants are added to make processed foods more appealing. Most colourings are derived from plants. There are also 20 permitted man-made colours. Caramel, E150, is the most used of the 52 permitted colourings.

Emulsifiers and stabilizers These chemical additives allow ingredients like oil and water to combine without separating. They make the texture of food smoother and more creamy, and help prevent baked foods from going stale.

Preservatives Chemicals in this category of additives protect food against the harmful effects of microbes which cause spoilage and food poisoning. They increase the storage life of foods.

Sweeteners These are added to food to improve its taste. Intense sweeteners are far sweeter than sugar and can be used in very small quantities. Bulk sweeteners have the same sweetness as sugar and are used in much the same way.

Food additives table

Antioxidants
EU approved*

E300	L-ascorbic acid
E301	sodium L-ascorbate
E302	calcium L-ascorbate
E304	6-0-palmitoyl-L-ascorbic acid (ascorbyl palmitate)

**Note:* Additives which have been approved by the European Union (EU) have a number with an E prefix. Additives which have been approved in the UK but are not EU-approved have a number without an E

Other food additives There are whole ranges of additional additives that are used in the preparation of food. These include acids, anti-caking agents, anti-foaming agents, bases, buffers, bulking agents, firming agents, flavour modifiers, flour improvers, glazing agents, humectants, liquid freezants, packaging gases, propellants, release agents, sequestrants and solvents.

Food additives table

The table below will help you identify particular additives from their name, number or E number. They are listed according to function. Those without a number are awaiting EU approval but are accepted in the UK (*see* **E numbers**, p. 228).

Antioxidants (continued)

EU approved*

E306	extracts of natural origin rich in tocopherols
E307	synthetic alpha-tocopherol
E308	synthetic gamma-tocopherol

continued

prefix. Some UK-approved additives have a name only and will not be given a number until they have been approved by the EU.

Food additives table (continued)

Antioxidants (continued)

EU approved*

E309	synthetic delta-tocopherol
E310	propyl gallate
E311	octyl gallate
E312	dodecyl gallate
E320	butylated hydroxyanisole (BHA)
E321	butylated hydroxytoluene (BHT)

UK approved*

	diphenylamine
	ethoxyquin

Colours

EU approved*

E100	curcumin
E101	riboflavin
E102	tartrazine
E104	quinoline yellow
E110	sunset yellow FCF
E120	cochineal
E122	carmoisine
E123	amaranth
E124	Ponceau 4R
E127	erythrosine BS
E131	Patent blue V
E132	indigo carmine
E140	chlorophyll

*See note on p. 230

Colours (continued)
EU approved*

E141	copper complexes of chlorophyll and chlorophyllins
E142	green S
E150	caramel
E151	black PN
E153	carbon Black (vegetable carbon)
E160(a)	*alpha*-carotene; *beta*-carotene; *gamma*-carotene
E160(b)	annatto; bixin; norbixin
E160(c)	capsanthin; paprika extract
E160(d)	lycopene
E160(e)	*beta*-apo-8'-carotenal
E160(f)	ethyl ester of beta-apo-8'-carotenoic acid
E161(a)	flavoxanthin
E161(b)	lutein
E161(c)	cryptoxanthin
E161(d)	rubixanthin
E161(e)	violaxanthin
E161(f)	rhodoxanthin
E161(g)	canthaxanthin
E162	beetroot red (betanin)
E163	anthocyanins
E171	titanium dioxide
E172	iron oxides; iron hydroxides
E173	aluminium
E174	silver
E175	gold
E180	pigment rubine (lithol rubine BK)

continued

Food additives table (continued)

Colours (continued)
UK approved*

128	red 2G
133	Brilliant Blue FCF
154	brown FK
155	brown HT
	riboflavin-5'-phosphate

Emulsifiers and stabilizers
EU approved*

E322	lecithins
E400	alginic acid
E401	sodium alginate
E402	potassium alginate
E403	ammonium alginate
E404	calcium alginate
E405	propane-1, 2-diol alginate (propylene glycol alginate)
E406	agar
E407	carrageenan
E410	locust bean gum (carob gum)
E412	guar gum
E413	tragacanth
E414	gum arabic (acacia)
E415	xanthan gum
E416	karaya gum
E440	(i) pectin
E440	(ii) amidated pectin
E460	(i) microcrystalline cellulose

*See note on p. 230

Emulsifiers and stabilizers (continued)
EU approved*

E461	methylcellulose
E463	hydroxypropylcellulose
E464	hydroxypropylmethylcellulose
E465	ethylmethylcellulose
E466	carboxymethlycellulose, sodium salt (CMC)
E470	sodium, potassium and calcium salts of fatty acids
E471	mono- and di-glycerides of fatty acids
E472(a)	acetic acid esters of mono- and di-glycerides of fatty acids
E472(b)	lactic acid esters of mono- and di-glycerides of fatty acids
E472(c)	citric acid esters of mono- and di-glycerides of fatty acids
E472(d)	tartaric acid esters of mono- and di-glycerides of fatty acids
E472(e)	mono- and diacetyltartaric acid esters of mono- and di-glycerides of fatty acids
E472(f)	mixed acetic and tartaric acid esters of mono- and di-glycerides of fatty acids
E473	sucrose esters of fatty acids
E474	sucroglycerides
E475	polyglycerol esters of fatty acids
E476	polyglycerol esters of polycondensed fatty acids of castor oil (polyglycerol polyricinoleate)

continued

Food additives table (continued)

Emulsifiers and stabilizers (continued)

EU approved*

E477	propane-1, 2-diol esters of fatty acids
E481	sodium stearoyl-2-lactylate
E482	calcium stearoyl-2-lactylate
E483	stearyl tartrate

UK approved*

432	polyoxyethelene (20) sorbitan monolaurate (polysorbate 20)
433	polyoxyethylene (20) sorbitan mono-oleate (polysorbate 80)
434	polyoxyethylene (20) sorbitan monopalmitate (polysorbate 40)
435	polyoxyethylene (20) sorbitan monostearate (polysorbate 60)
436	polyoxyethylene (20) sorbitan tristearate (polysorbate 65)
442	ammonium phosphatides
491	sorbitan monostearate
492	sorbitan tristearate
493	sorbitan monolaurate
494	sorbitan mono-oleate
495	sorbitan monopalmitate
	extract of quillaia
	oxidatively polymerised soya bean oil

*See note on p. 230

Emulsifiers and stabilizers (continued)
UK approved*

	pectin extract
	polyglycerol esters of dimerised fatty acids of soya bean oil

Preservatives
EU approved*

E200	sorbic acid
E201	sodium sorbate
E202	potassium sorbate
E203	calcium sorbate
E210	benzoic acid
E211	sodium benzoate
E212	potassium benzoate
E213	calcium benzoate
E214	ethyl 4-hydroxybenzoate (ethyl para-hydroxybenzoate)
E215	ethyl 4-hydroxybenzoate, sodium salt (sodium ethyl para-hydroxybenzoate)
E216	propyl 4-hydroxybenzoate (propyl para-hydroxybenzoate)
E217	propyl 4-hydroxybenzoate, sodium salt (sodium propyl para-hydroxybenzoate)
E218	methyl 4-hydroxybenzoate (methyl para-hydroxybenzoate
E219	methyl 4-hydroxybenzoate, sodium salt (sodium methyl para-hydroxybenzoate)
E220	sulphur dioxide

continued

Food additives table (continued)

Preservatives (continued)

EU approved*

E221	sodium sulphite
E222	sodium hydrogen sulphite (sodium bisulphite)
E223	sodium metabisulphite
E224	potassium metabisulphite
E226	calcium sulphite
E227	calcium hydrogen sulphite (calcium bisulphite)
E228	potassium bisulphite
E230	biphenyl (diphenyl)
E231	2-hydroxybiphenyl (orthophenylphenol)
E232	sodium biphenyl-2-yl oxide (sodium orthophenylphenate)
E233	2-(thiazol-4-yl) benzimidazole (thiabendazole)
E239	hexamine (hexamethylenetramine)
E249	potassium nitrite
E250	sodium nitrite
E251	sodium nitrate
E252	potassium nitrate
E280	propionic acid
E281	sodium propionate
E282	calcium propionate
E283	potassium propionate

UK approved*

234	nisin

*See note on p. 230

Sweeteners

EU approved*

E241	mannitol
E420	sorbitol; sorbitol syrup

UK approved*

acesulfame potassium
aspartame
hydrogenated glucose syrup
isomalt
lactitol
saccharin
calcium saccharin
sodium saccharin
thaumatin

Other additives

EU approved*

E170	calcium carbonate
E260	acetic acid
E261	potassium acetate
E262	sodium hydrogen diacetate
E263	calcium acetate
E270	lactic acid
E290	carbon dioxide
E325	sodium lactate
E326	potassium lactate
E327	calcium lactate

continued

Food additives table (continued)

Other additives (continued)
EU approved*

E330	citric acid
E331	sodium dihydrogen citrate (monosodium citrate); disodium citrate; trisodium citrate
E332	potassium dihydrogen citrate (monopotassium citrate); tripotassium citrate
E333	monocalcium citrate; dicalcium citrate; tricalcium citrate
E334	L-(+)-tartaric acid
E335	monosodium L-(+)-tartrate; disodium L-(+) tartrate
E336	monopotassium L-(+)-tartrate (cream of tartar); dipotassium L-(+)-tartrate
E337	potassium sodium L-(+)-tartrate
E338	orthophosphoric acid (phosphoric acid)
E339	sodium dihydrogen orthophosphate; disodium hydrogen orthophosphate; trisodium orthophosphate
E340	potassium dihydrogen orthophosphate; dipotassium hydrogen orthophosphate; tripotassium orthophosphate
E341	calcium tetrahydrogen diorthophosphate; calcium hydrogen orthophosphate; tricalcium diorthophosphate
E422	glycerol
E450(a)	disodium dihydrogen diphosphate; trisodium diphosphate; tetrasodium diphosphate; tetrapotassium diphosphate

*See note on p. 230

Other additives (continued)

EU approved*

E450(b)	pentasodium triphosphate; pentapotassium triphosphate
E450(c)	sodium polyphosphates, potassium polyphosphates
E460	(ii) alpha-cellulose (powdered cellulose)

UK approved*

262	sodium acetate
296	DL-malic acid; L-malic acid
297	fumaric acid
350	sodium malate; sodium hydrogen malate
351	potassium malate
352	calcium malate; calcium hydrogen malate
353	metatartaric acid
355	adipic acid
363	succinic acid
370	1,4-heptonolactone
375	nicotinic acid
380	triammonium citrate
381	ammonium ferric citrate
385	calcium disodium ethylenediamine-NNN'N'-tetra-acetate (calcium disodium EDTA)
500	sodium carbonate; sodium hydrogen carbonate (bicarbonate of soda); sodium sesquicarbonate

continued

Food additives table (continued)

Other additives (continued)

UK approved*

501	potassium bicarbonate; potassium hydrogen carbonate
503	ammonium carbonate; ammonium hydrogen carbonate
504	magnesium carbonate
507	hydrochloric acid
508	potassium chloride
509	calcium chloride
510	ammonium chloride
513	sulphuric acid
514	sodium sulphate
515	potassium sulphate
516	calcium sulphate
518	magnesium sulphate
524	sodium hydroxide
525	potassium hydroxide
526	calcium hydroxide
527	ammonium hydroxide
528	magnesium hydroxide
529	calcium oxide
530	magnesium oxide
535	sodium ferrocyanide
536	potassium ferrocyanide
540	dicalcium diphosphate
541	sodium aluminium phosphate
542	edible bone phosphate
544	calcium polyphosphates
545	ammonium polyphosphates
551	silicon dioxide (silica)

*See note on p. 230

Other additives (continued)
UK approved*

552	calcium silicate
553(a)	magnesium silicate synthetic; magnesium trisilicate
553(b)	talc
554	aluminium sodium silicate
556	aluminium calcium silicate
558	bentonite
559	kaolin
572	magnesium stearate
575	D-glucono-1, 5-lactone (glucono delta-lactone)
576	sodium gluconate
577	potassium gluconate
578	calcium gluconate
620	L-glutamic acid
621	sodium hydrogen L-glutamate (monosodium glutamate; MSG)
622	potassium hydrogen L-glutamate (monopotassium glutamate)
623	calcium dihydrogen di-L-glutamate (calcium glutamate)
627	guanosine 5'-disodium phosphate (sodium guanylate)
631	inosine 5'-disodium phosphate (sodium inosinate)
635	sodium 5'-ribonucleotide
900	dimethylpolysiloxane
901	beeswax

continued

Food additives table (continued)

Other additives (continued)
UK approved*

903	carnauba wax
904	shellac
905	mineral hydrocarbons
907	refined microcrystalline wax
920	L-cysteine hydrochloride
925	chlorine
926	chlorine dioxide
927	azodicarbonamide
	aluminium potassium sulphate
	2-aminoethanol
	ammonium dihydrogen orthophosphate; diammonium hydrogen othophosphate
	ammonium sulphate
	butyl stearate
	calcium heptonate
	calcium phytate
	dichlorodiflouromethane
	diethyl ether
	disodium dihydrogen ethylenediamine-NNN'N' (disodium dihydrogen EDTA)

FOOD LABELS

Datemarks

The law requires most food to carry a datemark. The most common datemarks are:

- **Best before** To enjoy food at its best, use by the date given. After the *Best before* date, the product is not

*See note on p. 230

Other additives (continued)
UK approved*

ethanol (ethylalcohol)
ethyl acetate
glycerol mono-acetate (monoacetin)
glycerol di-acetate (diacetin)
glycerol tri-acetate (triacetin)
glycine
hydrogen
nitrogen
nitrous oxide
octadecylammonium acetate
oxygen
oxystearin
polydextrose
propan-1, 2-diol (propylene glycol)
propan-2-ol (isopropyl alcohol)
sodium heptonate
spermaceti
sperm oil
tannic acid

dangerous but will no longer be at its best.

- **Use by** The product should be used by the date given. Food with this label is highly perishable but cooking or freezing before the *Use by* date can extend its life.

Some foods do not have to carry a datemark because it is clear when their quality is deteriorating (e.g. fresh fruit and vegetables) or because they have a very long life (e.g. vinegar and salt).

Ingredients

Ingredients, including additives, are listed on the label in descending order of the weight used in preparing the food. By law, most additives must be declared. *See* pp. 228–245 for more information on additives.

Nutritional information

This information helps us to make a healthier choice of food products. By law, companies need to give nutritional information if they are making a claim about the product, e.g. that it is low in calories or high in fibre. A claim such as 'reduced calorie' cannot be made unless the product is in fact much lower in calories than the normal version of the food.

Storage and preparation instructions

Ensure that storage, freezing, thawing, cooking and reheating instructions on food packages are followed. Use a thermometer to check that your fridge, freezer and cooker can maintain the recommended temperatures. These temperatures and times have been tested by food companies and will help to decrease the chance of food being infected by harmful bacteria.

A typical food label

Reduced sugar — Food claim

BAKED BEANS
in tomato sauce

INGREDIENTS

Beans, tomatoes, water, sugar (3%), modified starch, salt, onion powder, spices, vegetable oil, artificial sweetener (sodium saccharin) — Ingredients, including additives

DIRECTIONS

These beans are delicious hot or cold. To serve hot, empty contents into a saucepan. Stir gently until heated through.
Storage: Empty out unused contents, cover and keep cool. — Instructions for use and safe storage

NUTRITIONAL INFORMATION — Nutritional information

Typical values	per 100 g	per 200 g serving
Energy	252 kJ/ 60 kcal	504 kJ/ 120 kcal
Protein	5.2 g	10.4 g
Carbohydrate	10.5 g	21 g
(of which sugars	3 g	6 g)
Fat	0.5 g	1 g
(of which saturates	trace	trace)
Fibre	0.4 g	0.8 g
Sodium	5.5 g	11 g

Best before date on base of can — Datemark must appear on product

Made in London, England
by the manufacturer
Name of manufacturer
Full address of manufacturer — Name and address of the maker, packer or retailer

425 g e — Average weight (the **e** means that the weight of each pack may vary slightly)

BALANCING YOUR DIET

Tips for a healthy diet

What to eat

- Eat plenty of fresh vegetables and fruit.
- Reduce the amount of saturated fat in your diet by choosing lean meat, fish and poultry rather than fatty meat (*see* pp. 196–9 for information on fats).
- Choose low-fat dairy products.
- Beware of 'invisible' fats in products – check fat content on food labels.
- Increase your intake of starchy foods such as bread, pasta, cereals, rice and potatoes – these foods are low in fat and high in essential proteins, vitamins and minerals (*see* pp. 195–6 for information on starches).
- Use wholegrain versions of bread, pasta, cereals and rice; they have more fibre (*see* pp. 195–6).
- If your diet does not include meat, eat dairy products to ensure adequate intake of protein, or eat protein-rich meat substitutes (*see* p. 194).

Preparation and cooking

- Fry foods only occasionally and use unsaturated fats rather than saturates.
- Do not overcook or store food for long as vitamin levels drop.
- Do not soak vegetables – vitamins and minerals can dissolve away.
- Do not cut up vegetables long before they are to be used – exposure of cut surfaces causes vitamin and mineral levels to fall.
- Cook in as little water as possible, e.g. steam vegetables rather than boil.

Balancing your diet

The table below lists the five basic food groups and gives recommended daily servings of each needed for a healthy diet. The sixth category lists foods that should be restricted in a healthy diet.

Food group	Recommended number of servings **Examples of a serving**
Group 1	6–11 servings
Breads Cereals Rice Pasta	• 1 slice of bread • 30 g (1 oz) of dry breakfast cereal • 1/2 cup of cooked rice • 1/2 cup of cooked pasta
Group 2	3–5 servings
Vegetables	• 1 cup* of leafy greens • 1/2 cup* of a range of other kinds of vegetables
Group 3	2–4 servings
Fruits	• 1 medium apple, orange or banana • 3/4 cup of juice • 1/2 cup of diced fruit

continued

*Note: These measures are for raw quantities.

Balancing your diet (continued)

Food group	Recommended number of servings **Examples of a serving**
Group 4	2–3 servings
Meats Poultry Pulses Fish Nuts Eggs	• Small servings of each for a daily total of about 170 g (6 oz)* *Note:* The total should be increased to about 200 g (7 oz)* if the diet includes a high proportion of pulses.
Group 5	2–3 servings
Dairy products	• 1 cup of milk • 1 cup of yoghurt • 45 g (1 1/2 oz) of cheese
Group 6	Eat sparingly
• High-fat snack foods (*see* pp. 196–9 for information about fats) • Sweets (*see* pp. 195–6 for information about sugars) • Salty foods (*see* pp. 208–9 for information about salt) • Alcoholic drinks (high in calories and low in nutrients)	

**Note:* These measures are for cooked quantities.

Index

Additives, food 228–45; table 230–45
Alcoholic drink: cooking with 187; measuring 177; types of 175–6; wine, buying 178–83; wine, storing and serving 183–7

Bakeware and moulds 73–6
Balancing your diet 248–50
Beans *see* Pulses
Bread, types of 159
Buying: eggs 153; fruit 129–30; game 95; meat 87; nuts 142; poultry 95; pulses 142; seafood 107–11; tinned foods 172; vegetables 129–31; wine 178–83

Calories and joules 218; calorie table, food and drink 219–28
Carbohydrates 195–6
Cheese, types of 154–6
Cholesterol 195, 197
Coffee, storing 192; types of 190–2
Conversions: Calories to joules 218; Celsius to Fahrenheit/gas mark 25; cup and spoon measures to imperial/metric 23; Weights and volumes: imperial to metric 14, 16, 21; metric to imperial 15, 17; metric to US customary 19; US customary to metric 18, 21; US to UK units 20
Cookers: electric 48–9; gas 50; microwave 51–2; solid fuel 52–3
Cooking: eggs 154; game 100–04; meat 90–3; pasta 167; poultry 100–02; pulses 143–4; rice 168–9; seafood 113–14; vegetables 138–9; with alcoholic drink 187; with herbs and spices 151; with oils 163
Cooking ingredients glossary 38–47
Cooking methods

glossary 26–37
Cups and spoonfuls: equivalents in metric/UK imperial/US customary units 23; measures for common ingredients 24; measuring with 22
Customary units (US): conversion to metric 18; conversion to UK imperial 20; cup and spoonful equivalents 23; liquid and dry measures 21

Dairy products: storing 156–8; types of cheese 154–6; types of egg 153; types of milk 151–2
Diet, balancing your 248–50
Drink *see* Alcoholic drink

E numbers *see* Additives
Eggs: boiling 154; buying 153; sizes and uses 154; types of 153
Equipment and utensils 48–80

Fats 196–9
Fish *see* Seafood
Flour, types of 160–1
Food and energy 218–28; calorie table 219–28; energy in different foods 218–19
Food labels 244–7
Food processing machines 60–1
Freezers 58–60
Freezing *see* Storing
Fruit: buying 129–30; preserving 136–8; storing 134–6; types of 124–9

Game: buying 95; cooking 100–04; gaming seasons 95–6; hanging times 97; storing 98; thawing 99–100; types of 95
Glossaries: cooking ingredients 38–47; cooking methods 26–37

Hand tools 76–80
Health and nutrition 193–250; nutritional information on food labels 246
Herbs and spices: buying 150; cooking with 151;

storing 150–1; types of 144–50

Imperial units (UK): conversion to metric 14, 16; conversion to US customary 20; cup and spoonful equivalents 23; liquid and dry measures 21

Knives/cutting tools 69–72

Liquids *see* Volumes

Measuring: equipment 62–4; weights and volumes 12–24
Meat: buying 87; cooking 90–3; cuts of 82–6; storing 87–8; substitutes 171–2, 194; thawing 89
Metric units: conversion to UK imperial 15, 17; conversion to US customary 19; cup and spoonful equivalents 23–4
Milk: equivalents 152; types of 151–2
Minerals 208–17; major minerals 210–13; trace minerals 214–17

Nutrition *see* Health and nutrition
Nuts: buying 142; storing 142; types of 140

Oil: smoking temperatures of 163; types of 161–3

Pasta: colours 166; cooking 167; types of 164–6
Pasteurization 151–2
Pots and pans 65–8
Poultry: buying 95; chicken sizes 94; cooking 100–02; storing 98; thawing 99; types of 93–4
Preserving fruit 136–8
Proteins 193–4
Pulses: buying 142; cooking 143–4; soaking 143; types of 141

Refrigerating *see* Storing
Refrigerators 54–7
Rice: cooking 168–9; types of 167–8
Roasting *see* Cooking

Salt (sodium) content of foods 209
Seafood: buying 107–11;

cooking 113–14; storing 111–12; thawing 112; types of 105–07
Shellfish *see* Seafood
Spices *see* Herbs
Spoonful measures *see* Cups and spoonfuls
Storing: dairy products 156–8; fruit 134–6; game 98; herbs and spices 150–1; meat 87–8; miscellaneous foods 172–5; nuts 142; poultry/game 98; pulses 142; seafood 111–12; vegetables 132; wine 183–4
Sweeteners: types of 169–71

Tea: storing 192 ; types of 188–90
Temperature: conversions 25; shelf temperatures in gas ovens 50; units of 25
Thawing: meat 89; poultry/game 99–100

US units *see* Customary units
Utensils *see* Equipment

Vegetables: buying 129–31; cooking 138–9; storing 132–3; types of 115–24
Vegetarian alternatives 171–2, 194
Vitamins 200–07; fat-soluble vitamins 206–7; water-soluble vitamins 202–05
Volumes: conversion tables 16–24; cup and spoonful equivalents 23–4; liquid and dry measures 21; units of volume 13; water weights 20

Weights: conversion tables 14–15; units of 12; water weights 20
Wine: allowing wine to breathe 185; buying 178–83; decanting 184–5; international quality classifications and wine terms 178–83; serving order 187; serving temperatures 185–6; storing 183–4; types of 176; which wine to serve 186